easy

Microsoft®
FrontPage® 2003

Ned Snell

que®

Contents

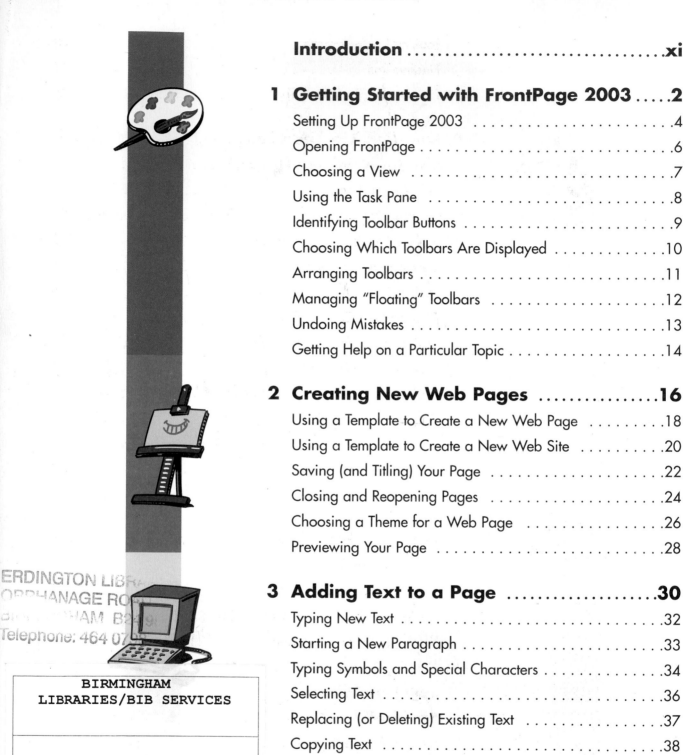

International Standard Book Number: 0-7897-2961-X

Library of Congress Catalog Card Number: 2003103670

Printed in the United States of America

First Printing: December 2003

05 04 03 02   4 3 2 1

Bulk Sales

Que Publishing offers excellent discounts on this book when ordered in quantity for bulk purchases or special sales. For more information, please contact:

U.S. Corporate and Government Sales

1-800-382-3419

corpsales@pearsontechgroup.com

For sales outside of the U.S., please contact:

International Sales

+1-317-428-3341

internationalsales@pearsontechgroup.com

Trademarks

All terms mentioned in this book that are known to be trademarks or service marks have been appropriately capitalized. Que Publishing cannot attest to the accuracy of this information. Use of a term in this book should not be regarded as affecting the validity of any trademark or service mark.

Warning and Disclaimer

Associate Publisher
Greg Wiegand

Acquisitions Editor
Michelle Newcomb

Development Editors
Laura Norman
Kate Shoup Welsh

Managing Editor
Charlotte Clapp

Project Editor
Tricia Liebig

Copy Editors
Geneil Breeze
Seth Kerney

Indexer
Kelly Castell

Technical Editor
Bill Bruns

Team Coordinator
Sharry L. Gregory

Interior Designer
Anne Jones

Cover Designer
Anne Jones

About the Author

Ned Snell has written more than two dozen computer books and hundreds of articles on computing technology. He is a research analyst for the Human Resource Institute, and he works as a professional actor in regional theater, commercials, and industrial films. He lives in Florida.

Dedication

For my family.

Acknowledgments

Thanks to the folks at Que—especially Michelle Newcomb and Kate Shoup Welsh.

We Want to Hear from You!

As the reader of this book, *you* are our most important critic and commentator. We value your opinion and want to know what we're doing right, what we could do better, what areas you'd like to see us publish in, and any other words of wisdom you're willing to pass our way.

As an associate publisher for Que, I welcome your comments. You can email or write me directly to let me know what you did or didn't like about this book—as well as what we can do to make our books better.

Please note that I cannot help you with technical problems related to the *topic* of this book. We do have a User Services group, however, where I will forward specific technical questions related to the book.

When you write, please be sure to include this book's title and author as well as your name, email address, and phone number. I will carefully review your comments and share them with the author and editors who worked on the book.

Email: feedback@quepublishing.com

Mail: Greg Wiegand
           Que Publishing
           800 East 96th Street
           Indianapolis, IN 46240 USA

For more information about this book or another Que title, visit our Web site at www.quepublishing.com. Type the ISBN (excluding hyphens) or the title of a book in the Search field to find the page you're looking for.

1 Each step is fully illustrated to show you how it looks onscreen.

It's as Easy as 1-2-3
Each part of this book is made up of a series of short, instructional lessons, designed to help you understand basic information that you need to get the most out of your computer hardware and software.

2 Each task includes a series of quick, easy steps designed to guide you through the procedure.

3 Items that you select or click in menus, dialog boxes, tabs, and windows are shown in **bold**.

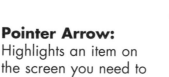

Looking Up Synonyms

Start

1 Click

2 Click **3** Click **4** Click

1 After you select the word for which you want to see synonyms, open the **Tools** menu and choose **Thesaurus**.

2 The Thesaurus dialog box opens. If two or more choices are in the **Meanings** list, click the one that most closely matches the meaning you want.

3 In the **Replace with Synonym** list, click the word you want to use.

4 Click the **Replace** button to close the thesaurus and replace your original word with the synonym.

End

Another feature of FrontPage is the built-in thesaurus that can suggest some synonyms, alternative words with the same meaning, for text that you've typed.

Canceling the Thesaurus
If you don't like any of the suggested synonyms better than your original word, click **Cancel** in the Thesaurus dialog box to close it.

Finding More Choices
To display a new list of synonyms based on one of the suggestions in the Replace with Synonym list, click the suggestion and then click the **Look Up** button.

Introductions explain what you will learn in each task and **Tips and Hints** give you a heads-up for any extra information you may need while working through the task.

Drag

Drop

How to Drag:
Point to the starting place or object. Hold down the mouse button (right or left per instructions), move the mouse to the new location, then release the button.

See next page

See next page:
If you see this symbol, it means the task you're working on continues on the next page.

End

End Task:
Task is complete.

Selection:
Highlights the area onscreen discussed in the step or task.

Click:
Click the left mouse button once.

Right-click:
Click the right mouse button once.

Click & Type:
Click once where indicated and begin typing to enter your text or data.

Double-click:
Click the left mouse button twice in rapid succession.

Pointer Arrow:
Highlights an item on the screen you need to point to or focus on in the step or task.

Introduction to *Easy Microsoft FrontPage 2003*

If it's an easy Web-authoring experience you're looking for, you've already done two things right. The first was choosing FrontPage 2003 as your Web-authoring program. There are other programs, but none that let you create really professional looking pages and entire Web sites as easily.

Your second smart step in keeping things easy was picking up this book. Here, you'll find not only clear, simple steps for using FrontPage 2003 to create Web pages and make them look great, but also help with developing whole Web sites and publishing your pages and sites.

All you need to get started is your PC, access to the Internet, and FrontPage 2003 itself. (It's okay if you've already installed FrontPage 2003, but if you haven't, you'll learn how in Part 1, "Getting Started with FrontPage 2003.") Got all that? Okay, then it's time to get started...

Getting Started with FrontPage 2003

Like all better Web-authoring programs, FrontPage 2003 is described as a *WYSIWYG (what you see is what you get)* program, because while you're working on a Web page, the program shows you what the page will look like online. A WYSIWYG Web-authoring program enables you to create a Web page in much the same way you would create a letter, brochure, or flyer on a word processor.

Then again, a Web-authoring program is not exactly like any word processor you might already have met. So before diving into creating pages (as you'll do in Part 2, "Creating New Web Pages"), it's smart to spend a few minutes now exploring the FrontPage program. This orientation will make everything that follows it even easier.

The FrontPage Window

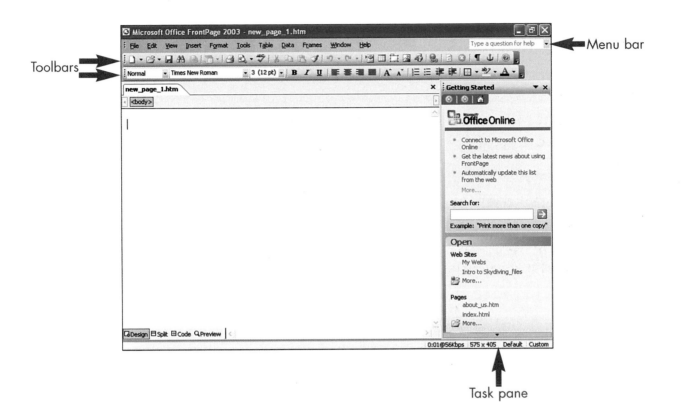

Setting Up FrontPage 2003

Start

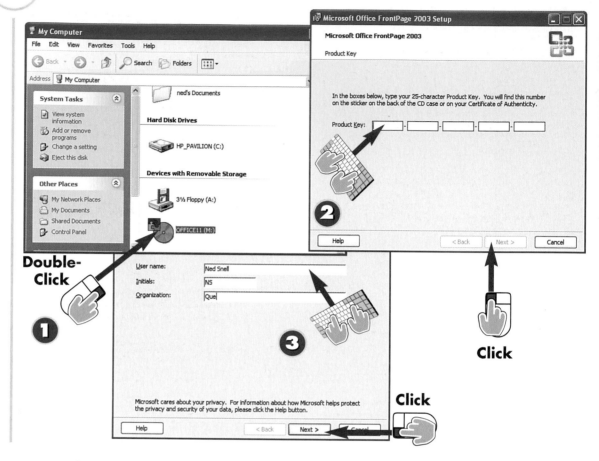

Double-Click

①

Click

Click

③

②

① Insert the FrontPage 2003 CD-ROM. Wait for Setup to start automatically. (If it doesn't, open your **My Computer** folder and double-click the **CD icon**.)

② In the **Product Key** fields, type the product key that appears on the sticker that came with your FrontPage 2003 packaging, and then click **Next**.

③ Type the requested information in the **User name** field (any name you want), **Initials**, and, optionally, **Organization** fields. Then click **Next**.

INTRODUCTION

FrontPage is a snap to install. If you've set up other Windows programs, you'll find installing FrontPage easy and familiar. (If you've already installed FrontPage 2003, skip to the next task.)

TIP

System Requirements
FrontPage 2003 requires Windows XP (recommended) or Windows 2000 (with Service Pack 3 or later installed) on a Pentium PC (133MHz or higher) with at least 64MB of memory (128MB recommended) and at least 245MB of free disk space.

HINT

Windows 2000
The screen images in this book show FrontPage 2003 running in Windows XP, but it'll work the same in Windows 2000. That means all the steps you learn here will work fine for Windows 2000, too.

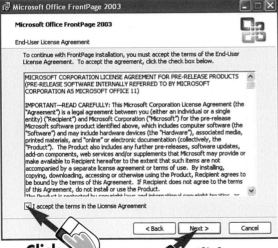

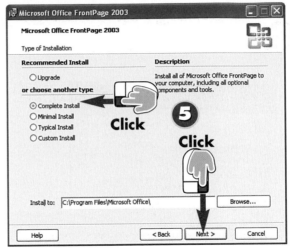

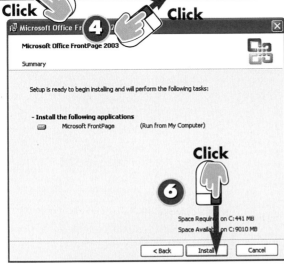

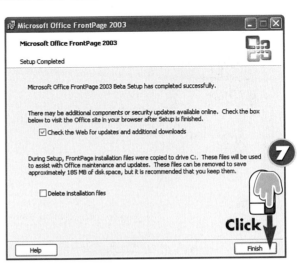

4 Click the **I accept the terms in the License Agreement** check box to select it, and then click **Next**.

5 Choose **Complete Install** to install all of FrontPage's features and files; choose **Typical Install** to install only the most used features. Then click **Next**.

6 Click the **Install** button. FrontPage might lead you through several more screens to complete the installation; just follow the prompts to finish up.

7 When FrontPage reports that Setup is finished, click **Finish**, and then click **Yes** when prompted to restart Windows.

HINT

Do I Need the CD?
After setup, the CD-ROM need not be in your PC when you use FrontPage. Some activities—such as inserting *clip art* (see Part 6)—might require the CD-ROM, but when you begin these activities, FrontPage reminds you to insert it.

TIP

Custom Install
In step 5, you can choose **Custom Install** to choose which parts of FrontPage to install and which to ignore. But most users—and *all* beginners—should rely on either **Complete Install** or **Typical Install**.

Opening FrontPage

Start

Click

Click

Click

Click

Click

1 Click the Windows **Start** button.

2 Click **All Programs** (in Windows 2000, it's just **Programs**).

3 Click **Microsoft Office**, and then click **Microsoft Office FrontPage 2003**.

4 To close FrontPage 2003, click the **Close** (×) button in the upper-right corner of the FrontPage window.

End

INTRODUCTION

Here's how to get FrontPage 2003 open and ready for work. When FrontPage opens for the first time, it automatically opens a new, blank Web page file. You can start typing right away to begin creating a Web page—although in Part 2, you'll discover better ways to get a new page going.

HINT

Closing FrontPage

You can close FrontPage by opening the **File** menu and then choosing **Exit**, or by clicking the **Close** (×) button in the upper-right corner of the FrontPage window.

Choosing a View

Start

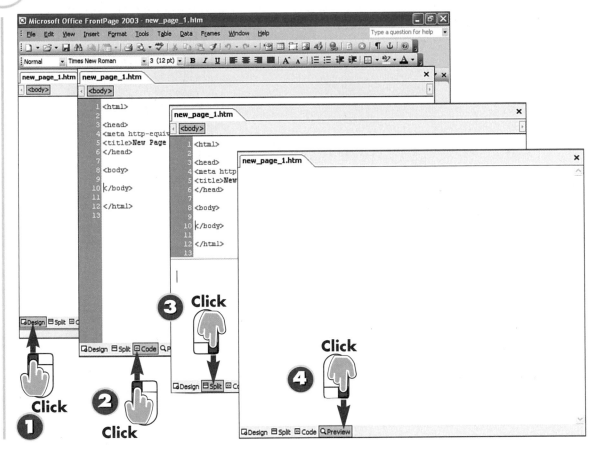

③ Click

Click

④

Click

Click

① Click

② Click

① Click the **Design** button to open the space in Page view, which you use to create, edit, and format the contents of your page.

② Click the **Code** button to see (and, optionally, edit) the actual raw HTML code of the page you're creating.

③ Click the **Split button** to split the screen and display the page's code in a window on top and the working page in a window on the bottom.

④ Click the **Preview** button to see how the page will appear when viewed through a Web browser (see Part 2).

End

INTRODUCTION

FrontPage 2003 offers different windows, or *views*, each of which is used for a different type of activity. FrontPage automatically puts you in the view you need when you start a given task, so typically, you needn't think about views. (If you want to switch to a different view than the one FrontPage has you in, just open the View menu and choose a view from the menu that appears.) When creating and editing Web pages, you'll work mostly in Page view. The other views are for managing Web sites (multiple pages that work together), which you'll explore in later chapters.

Using the Task Pane

Start

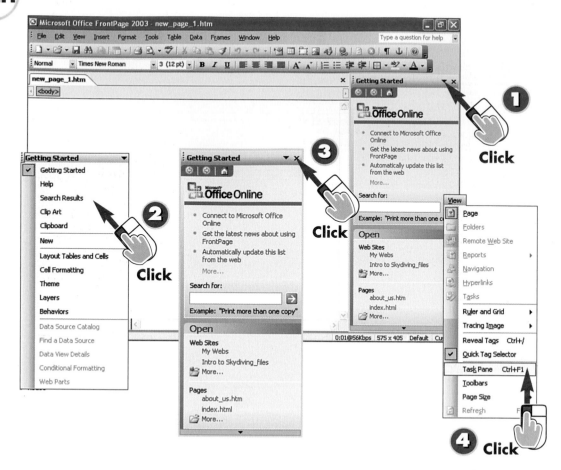

Click

Click

Click

Click

1 To choose from the different task-oriented content the task pane can display, click the small **down arrow** in the task pane's upper-right corner (next to the **Close** (×) button).

2 From the menu that appears, choose the content you want to see.

3 To close the task pane, click the Close (×) button in the task pane's upper-right corner.

4 To redisplay the task pane after having closed it, open the **View** menu and select **View Task Pane**.

End

Identifying Toolbar Buttons

Start

1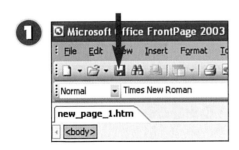

2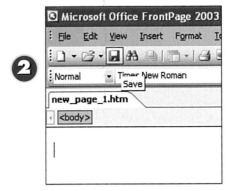

1 Using your mouse, point to the button whose name you want to know—but don't click.

2 Wait a moment without moving the mouse, and the button's name appears.

End

You perform many activities in FrontPage by clicking buttons on the *toolbars* that appear near the top of the window. The pictures in this book will help you easily identify and locate the toolbar button you need for any task, but it's also handy to know how to display ScreenTips to learn the name of any button on a toolbar.

Displaying the Names of a Whole Row of Buttons
To easily review the names on a whole row of buttons, point to the first button in the row and wait for its ScreenTip to appear. Then slowly move the pointer to the right, along the row, without pausing. As the pointer passes each button, the button's name appears.

Choosing Which Toolbars Are Displayed

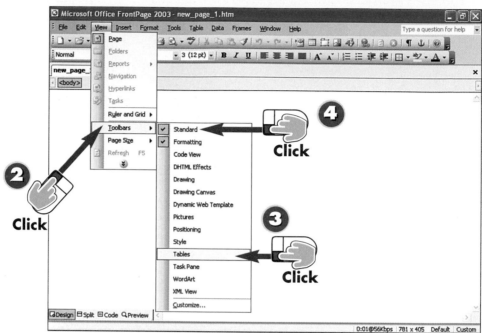

Standard toolbar

Formatting toolbar

Click

Click

Click

1 FrontPage displays the Standard and Formatting toolbars at first, by default.

2 Open the **View** menu and choose **Toolbars**. In the submenu that appears, you'll see a check mark next to the name of each toolbar currently displayed.

3 To display a toolbar that's not checked, click its name in the submenu.

4 To hide a toolbar that is checked, click its name in the submenu.

End

You perform most Web-page authoring activities with two main toolbars: Standard and Formatting. But FrontPage actually has more toolbars, most of which appear automatically when you need them and disappear when you don't. Still, anytime you need a particular toolbar and don't see it, you can make it appear.

TIP

Customizing Toolbars
To the far right of each toolbar, a tiny arrow appears. If you click that arrow and then click the button that appears, you can choose which tools appear on the toolbar. You can customize the toolbars to your precise needs.

Arranging Toolbars

Start

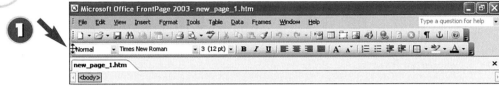

1

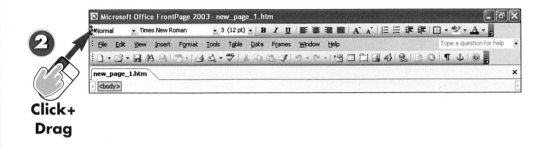

2

Click+
Drag

1 Using your mouse, point to the vertical bar at the extreme left end of the toolbar you want to move.

2 Click and hold on the **vertical bar**, and then drag the toolbar up or down in the toolbar area to its new position.

3 Release the mouse button. The toolbar is moved.

End

INTRODUCTION

Besides hiding and displaying them, you can move and rearrange FrontPage's toolbars in their docked positions above the work area to change the order in which they're shown. You might find that using the toolbars is more convenient if you rearrange their order in a way that best fits the way you work.

TIP

Toolbar Overlap
If you see a double-arrow symbol (>>) in the middle of a toolbar row, two toolbars are overlapping. Clicking that symbol reveals the tools hidden by the overlapping. To fix the overlap, drag either toolbar just slightly up or down.

HINT

You Can Move the Menu Bar, Too
You can also change the position of the FrontPage menu bar, following these same steps. For example, you can move the menu bar below the toolbars or between them.

Managing "Floating" Toolbars

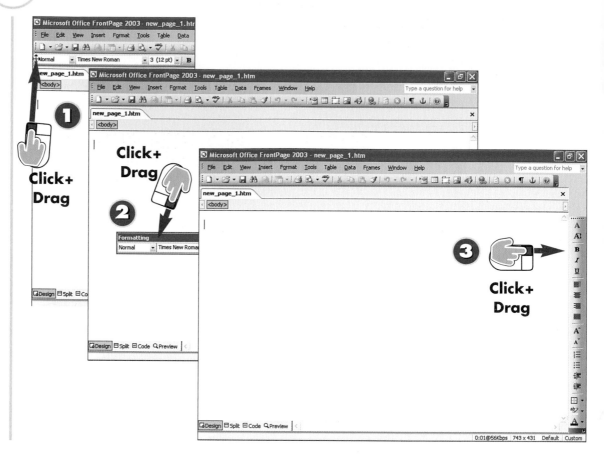

1. To float a docked toolbar, click and hold on its vertical bar, drag it onto the work area, and then release the mouse button.

2. To move a floating toolbar out of your way, click and hold on its title bar (where you see its name), and then drag it where you want it.

3. To dock a toolbar on the side or bottom of the screen, drag it all the way to the side or bottom.

INTRODUCTION

A *floating toolbar* appears as a box of tools anywhere in the FrontPage window, not as a row in the toolbar area. You can float any toolbar (or even the menu bar), and drag a floating toolbar anywhere in the work area. Some floating toolbars appear automatically when needed, but you can dock those, too.

TIP

Some Toolbars Start at the Bottom

Some toolbars, such as the Picture toolbar (see Part 6), pop up docked but not in the toolbar area—they dock below the work area. Note that you can float these, too, or dock them in the toolbar area or on the sides.

HINT

Fast-Docking

To easily dock a floating toolbar in the last place it was previously docked, double-click its title bar.

Undoing Mistakes

Start

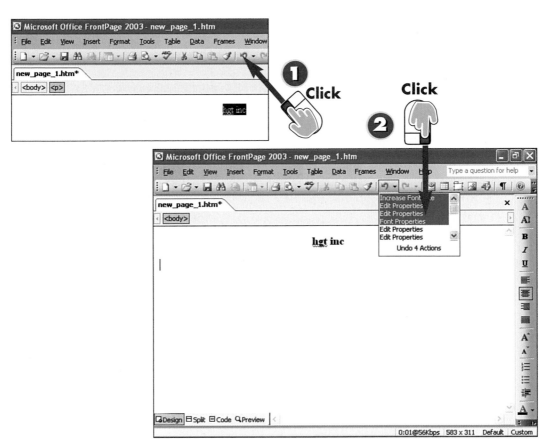

Click **Click**

1 Right after performing any action you regret, click the **Undo** button on the Standard toolbar to reverse that action. Keep clicking **Undo** to reverse previous actions one by one.

2 If you're not sure how many times to click Undo, click the **Undo** button's **down arrow** to open a list of recent actions, and then click the action you want to undo.

End

INTRODUCTION

Here's as good a place as any to point out FrontPage's handy *Undo* feature. If you delete some text or a picture and then suddenly realize that you want it back, you can use Undo to retrieve it.

TIP

Undo Takes Your Page Backward in Time
When you click **Undo** several times to undo an action you made a little while ago, you undo not only that action, but *everything you've done since*. In effect, you take the page back in time to the moment before you goofed.

Getting Help on a Particular Topic

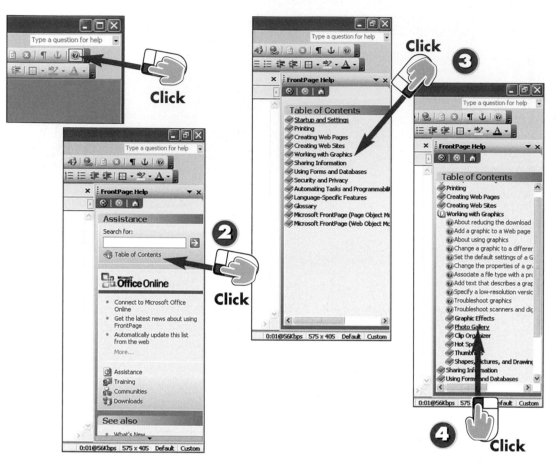

1 Click the **Microsoft Office FrontPage Help** button on the Standard toolbar, or press the **F1** key on your keyboard. The Microsoft FrontPage Help task pane opens.

2 In the task pane, click **Table of Contents**.

3 Scroll through the list of topics, and click one that appears related to what you want help with.

4 Scroll through the list of help articles, and click the one that looks like it might hold your answers.

Some Help Requires the Internet

FrontPage 2003 pulls some of its help material from the Web. If your Internet connection is not open when you click Table of Contents, you might be prompted to connect to the Internet before continuing.

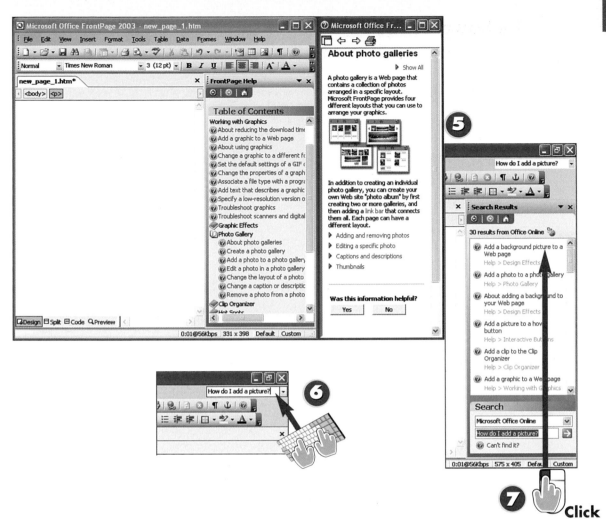

Click

5 Read the Help text displayed in the task pane.

6 Alternatively, you can type your question in the **Type a question for help** box at the right end of the menu bar and press Enter.

7 Scroll through the list of help topics and click the one that looks like it might have the answer to read the help text.

End

Phrasing a Question for Help
When phrasing a question for Help, don't worry about capitalization, but do avoid contractions (type "what is" rather than "what's").

Printing Help
To print the Help topic you're reading, click the **Print** button atop the help window.

Creating New Web Pages

Nothing is more discouraging than staring at a blank page and knowing that you have to find a way to fill it up. Fortunately, when you use FrontPage 2003, you can take advantage of a variety of tools that help you go from blank to beautiful in just a few clicks.

In this part, you'll learn how to get a head start on creating Web pages (and entire Web sites) by basing them on *templates*, which are predesigned pages that you can make your own by replacing their sample dummy content with your own words and pictures.

Templates save time, but they present a funny problem for a FrontPage beginner. When you start a page or site this way, you might get a file that contains all sorts of objects (pictures, buttons, links) and formatting (tables, fonts, backgrounds) that you haven't learned to manipulate yet.

It's nothing to worry about. Just keep in mind that when you use a template, you might not understand exactly how to deal with all of your page's predefined objects and formatting until you get farther along in this book.

Don't worry about making a choice that looks exactly right; you'll find it's easy to change the visual style later, especially by changing the *theme* (see "Choosing a Theme for a Web Page" later in this part). Just look for a template with an overall layout that seems right for the type of content you want to put in it.

Creating New Pages

Page title/filename

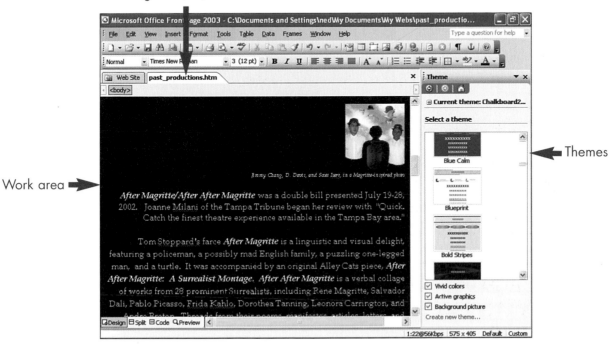

Work area

Themes

Using a Template to Create a New Web Page

Start

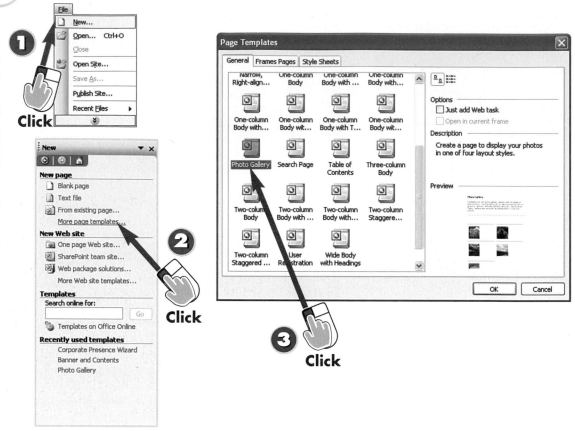

Click

Click

Click

1 Open the **File** menu and choose **New**.

2 The New task pane opens. Click the **More page templates** link in the New Page section of the task pane to start a new, single Web page.

3 The Page Templates dialog box opens. Click each of the template icons in the **General** tab, and watch the **Preview** area.

Starting Quick with the Blank Page

TIP

If you feel like creating a page from scratch, start off by working with the empty page that appears automatically whenever you open FrontPage—click the **Create a New Normal Page** button.

Getting Templates from the Net

TIP

Notice the **Search online for** search box above the Other templates area on the task pane. If your computer has an active Internet connection, you can use this search box to search for and use many more templates.

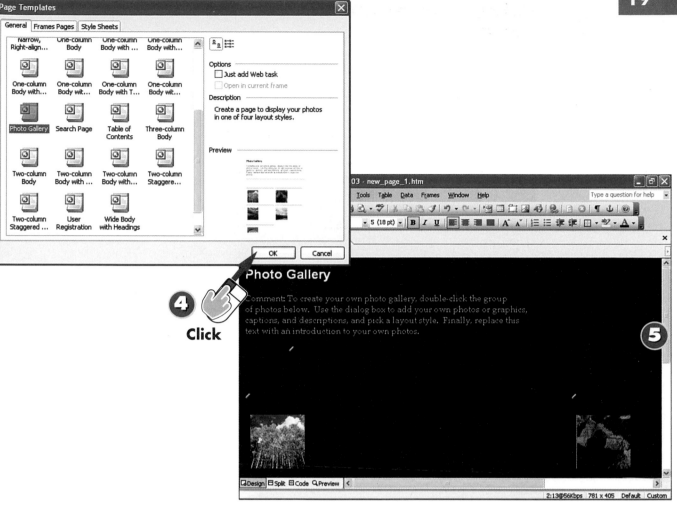

Click

4 When the page you see in the Preview area is a good match for the style and layout of the page you want to create, click **OK**.

5 A page based on the template you selected is created and displayed onscreen. To save the page and give it a title, see "Saving (and Titling) Your Page."

End

You Can Change *Anything* in a Template
After creating a page, you can edit and enhance its content and design any way you want by following the steps shown throughout the rest of this book. You can even change or remove any of the objects or formatting the template put there—the file is all yours now.

Using a Template to Create a New Web Site

Start

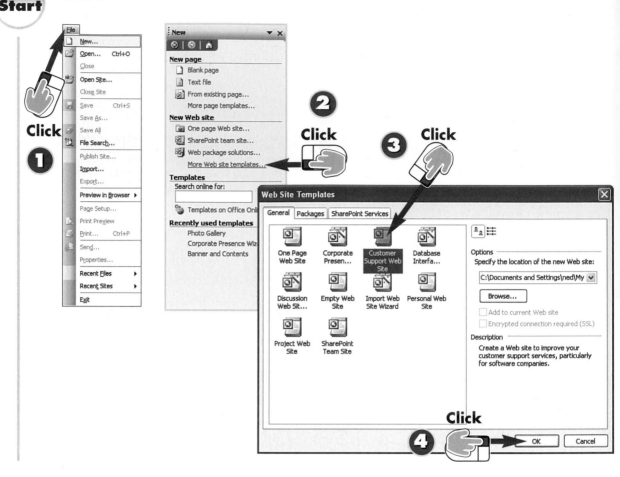

Click ①

Click ②

Click ③

Click ④

① Open the **File** menu and choose **New**.

② The New task pane opens. Click the **More Web site templates** link in the Other templates section of the task pane to start a new Web site.

③ The Web Site Templates dialog box opens. One by one, click each of the Web site icons in the **General** tab, and read a description of the template in the Template area.

④ When the description shown is the best available match for the type of site you want to create, click **OK**.

TIP

Using "Wizards"
If the name of the icon you select in step 3 ends in "Wizard," you will be asked a simple series of questions that FrontPage uses to tailor the new Web site to your needs. After you answer (or skip) the questions, view the Web site as described in step 5.

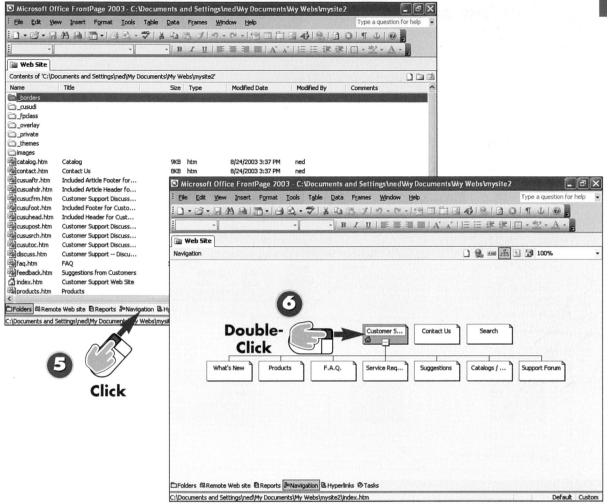

⑤ A Web site based on the template is created. In the Views bar, click the **Navigation** button to switch to Navigation view, which displays a map of the pages.

⑥ To open a page in your Web site in Page view (so that you can edit it), double-click that page in the Navigation map.

End

Changing the Pages a Web Site Contains
A Web site starts out with a default organization and number of pages, but you can reorganize a site and add, delete, and move the pages within it. For details, see Part 9.

Saving (and Titling) Your Page

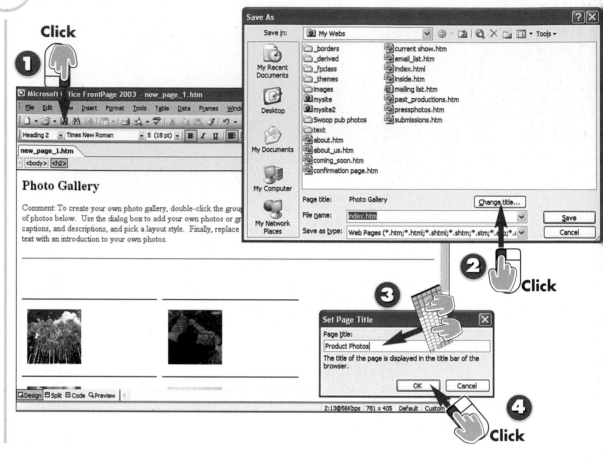

Start

Click

Click

Click

1. With the page you want to save displayed onscreen, click the **Save** button on the Standard toolbar.

2. The Save As dialog box opens. Click the **Change title** button.

3. The Set Page Title dialog box opens. Type a title for the page in the **Page title** field.

4. Click **OK**.

INTRODUCTION
When you save a new page, you choose not only its filename but also its *title*. The title of a Web page does not appear within the layout of the page itself, but in the title bar of the browser window. The title also helps identify your page to Web search tools.

TIP
Template-Based Pages Already Have Names
Pages in a Web site created from a template already have titles and filenames, so step 1 alone saves them. See Part 9 to learn how to change the title or filename of a page in a Web site.

TIP
Keep Titles Short...
Make your title short but also clear and descriptive. Avoid meaningless, overused titles such as "My Home Page," and try to work the most important, identifying keywords into the title—for example, "Harry Smith's Beer Recipes."

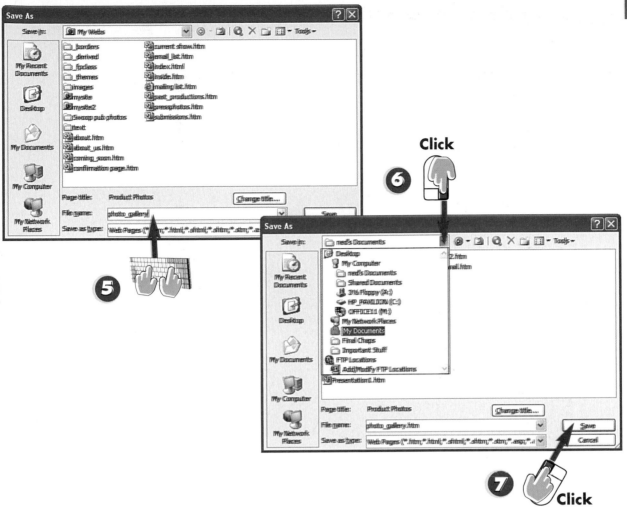

Click

6

5

7

Click

5 Back in the Save As dialog box, click in the **File name** text box, and type a short, descriptive filename.

6 Click the **down arrow** next to the **Save in** field and choose a folder in which to save this page from the list that appears.

7 Click the **Save** button to save the page and close the **Save As** dialog box.

End

Saving Guidelines

HINT
When typing a filename in step 5, do not type a filename extension (FrontPage adds .htm for you). Keep the name short and simple, and do not use any spaces or punctuation in the filename except dashes (-) or underscores (_).

Subsequent Saves

TIP
After the first time you save a page, you'll no longer need to perform steps 2–7 when you save again. Step 1 alone saves the file with the title, filename, and folder you've previously selected.

Closing and Reopening Pages

Start

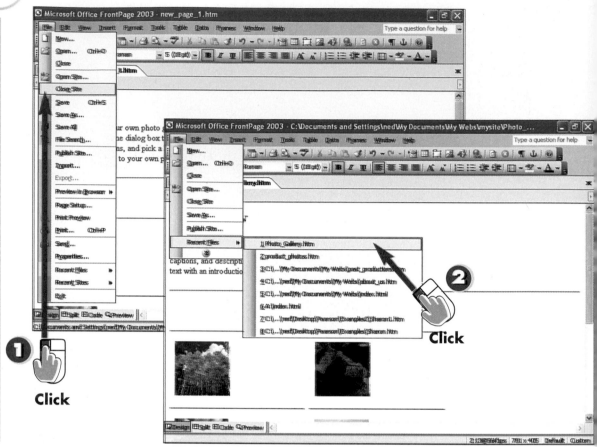

Click

Click

1 To close a page file (without closing FrontPage), open the **File** menu and choose **Close Site**.

2 To open one of the page files you've used recently, open the **File** menu, choose **Recent Files**, and then choose the page's filename from the submenu that appears.

As you work on Web pages, you'll probably create them over a series of editing sessions. You'll need to open existing pages and close them when you're finished.

Keeping Multiple Pages Open

TIP

If you open or create a page without first closing another page that's already open, you'll have both pages open at once. That's okay—you can keep two, three, or even more pages open and switch from working on one to any other by choosing a page's name from the Window menu.

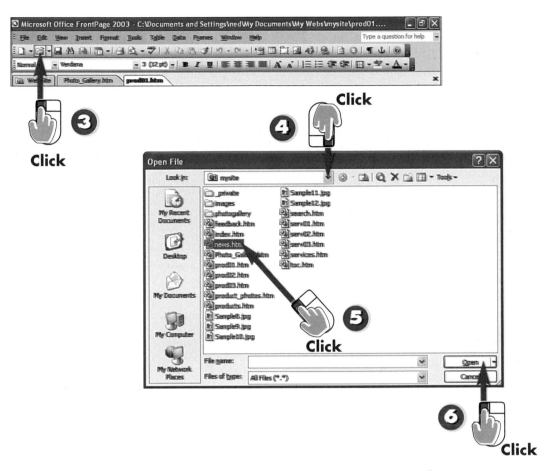

Click ③

Click ④

Click ⑤

Click ⑥

③ If a file you want is not among the files you've edited, it won't appear on the Recent Files submenu. In that case, click the **Open** button on the Standard toolbar.

④ In the Open File dialog box, click the **down arrow** next to the **Look in** field and choose the folder in which the page was saved.

⑤ When you see the page's filename listed among the files and folders shown in the dialog box, click the name to select it.

⑥ Click the **Open** button to open the page file.

End

Choosing a Theme for a Web Page

Start

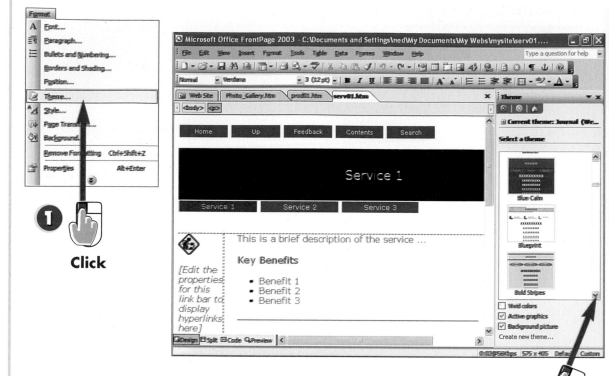

① **Click**

② **Click**

① While viewing your page in Design or Preview view, open the **Format** menu and choose **Theme**.

② The Theme task pane opens. Use the scroll arrows to scroll through the themes that are thumbnailed in the task pane to see what a sample page using that theme looks like.

The visual style of a Web page is determined by a variety of things: text *fonts* (typefaces) and colors, accent graphics, the background, and so on. A FrontPage *theme* is a way to choose all these page features at once. Choosing a theme not only saves time but also helps ensure that all these visual element choices work well together.

Ignore Layout When Using Themes
When previewing a theme, ignore the layout of the page shown in the sample. What the theme controls is not the organization of objects on the page, but rather the style of fonts, colors, buttons, and so on.

Themes Are Best for Sites
Themes are handy for single pages, but even handier for sites (see Part 9) because they let you change the style of some or all pages in a site at once. The steps are the same as adding a theme to a page.

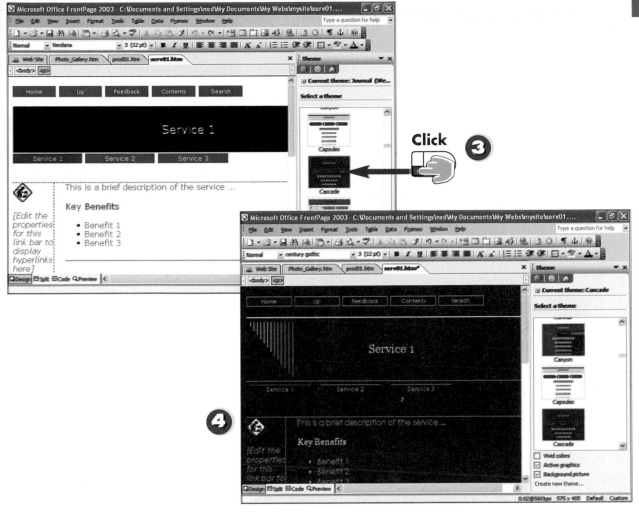

3 Click on the theme that shows the fonts, colors, and other stylistic elements that you want to use.

4 The theme you selected is applied to your page. Add to, edit, and develop your page as needed, saving often.

End

Previewing Your Page

Start

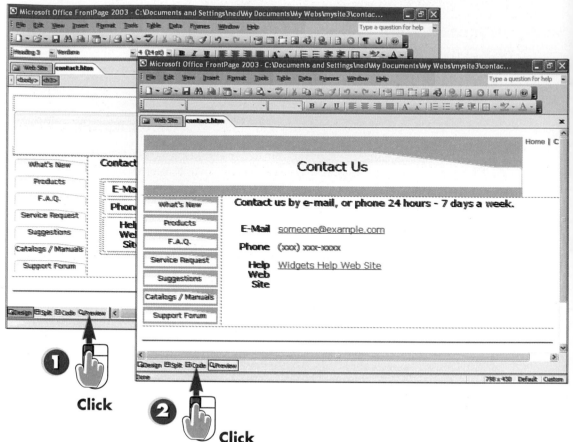

Click

1

2

Click

1 While viewing the page you want to preview, click the **Preview** button in the views bar.

2 The page is displayed as it will appear in your default Web browser. To return to normal working mode, click the **Design** button in the views bar.

INTRODUCTION

FrontPage shows your page to you as it will appear online—but not exactly. Some kinds of objects don't do their thing in Design view; for example, animations sit still. However, FrontPage offers two "preview options" to help you evaluate how your page will really look to visitors.

TIP

Different Browsers Show Different Results

It's impossible to create a page that looks exactly the same no matter which browser it's viewed through. Differences among browsers affect the look of even simple Web pages. Your FrontPage work will look just as you expect in Internet Explorer 6, but might look a little different in other browsers. Always test your work in multiple browsers (see Part 11, "Adding Fill-in-the-Blanks Forms") before publishing.

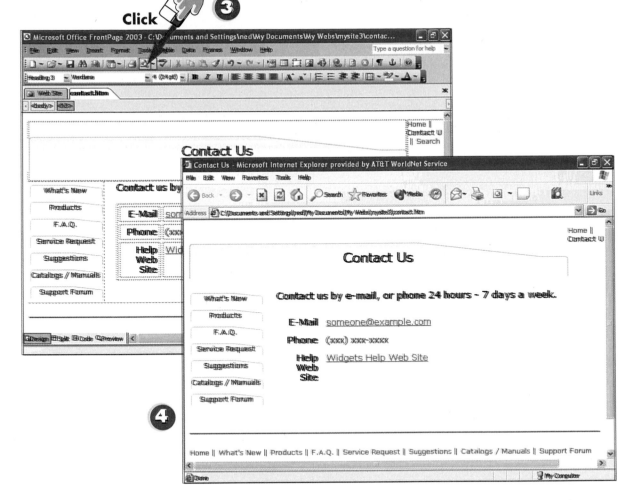

Click

3 To view the page in the default Web browser on your PC, click the **Preview** button on the Standard toolbar.

4 A separate browser window opens, displaying the Web page. To return to working in FrontPage, click the browser window's **Close** or **Minimize** button.

End

You Can Choose Your Preview Browser
If you have multiple browsers set up on your PC, you can choose which browser to preview the page in by clicking the **down arrow** next to the **Preview** button and choosing a browser from the list that appears. Doing this can help you make sure that your page looks good in any popular browser.

Save Before Previewing
You must already have saved any new changes to the page before previewing it in your browser. If you forget to do so, FrontPage reminds you when you click the **Preview** button.

Adding Text to a Page

Pretty soon, you'll start adding pictures to your page (or replacing pictures that the template put there). And by all means, pictures are important. But it's the words, or *text*, that carry most of your content. Text does the critical job of saying what you want your Web page to say. It might not always be the coolest thing on your pages, but it's usually the most important thing.

When you start with a blank page, the only place you can type new text is at the top of the page. After text or other objects are in the page, you can insert text in various spots within the page by clicking between objects to position the insertion point there.

In this part, you explore the ways you create, edit, and correct Web page text in FrontPage 2003. You'll find that the job is much like using a word processor—only easier. (And in Part 4, "Dressing Up Your Text," you'll learn how to make that text look sharp!)

Text Editing Tools

Spell-Checker   Copy   Paste

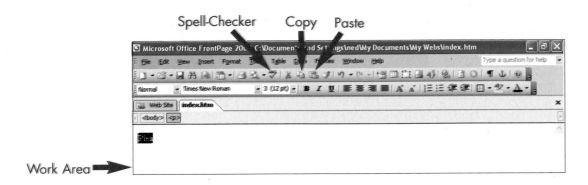

Work Area

Typing New Text

Start

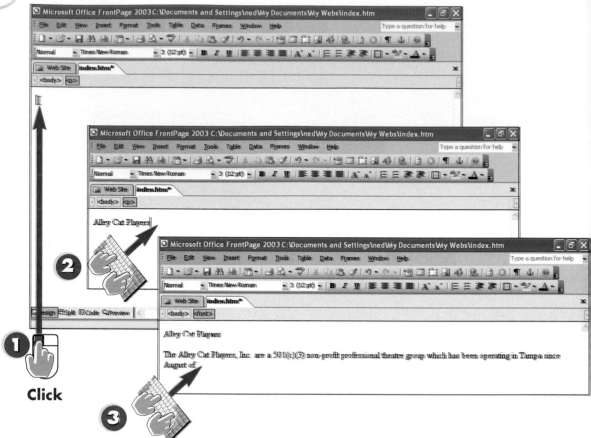

Click

---

1. Click the page at the spot where you want to add text. The insertion point, a flashing vertical bar, appears where you clicked.

2. Type your text.

3. When you reach the end of a line, keep typing—the insertion point jumps automatically to the next line causing the text to "wrap."

End

Got a hole in your page that needs filling with your thoughts? Just type away! As you begin entering text in your Web page, don't worry about what the text looks like. Just get the raw text typed in, and you can improve how it looks later.

Don't Forget to Save!
Don't forget to save your Web page file often, especially after adding or changing text. See "Saving (and Titling) Your Page" in Part 2 to learn how to save.

Starting a New Paragraph

Start

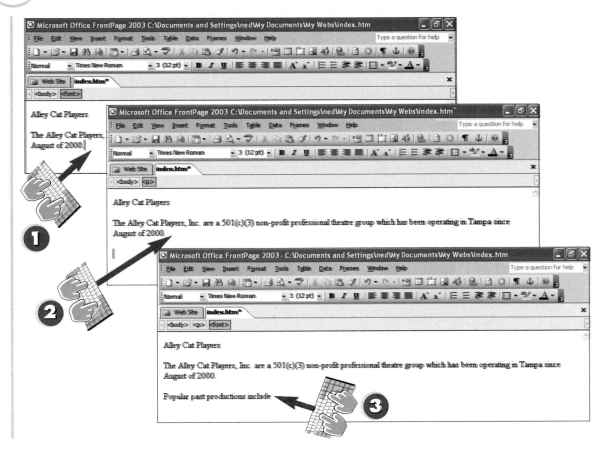

1 Type to the very end of a paragraph.

2 Press the **Enter** key on your keyboard. The insertion point drops away from the paragraph to a new, blank line, with an extra line automatically inserted.

3 Type the new paragraph.

End

Certain types of formatting—such as styles, indents, and alignments—always apply to a whole paragraph, *never* to only part of a paragraph. So where you choose to break paragraphs—end one and start another—has a big effect on how you can format the text they contain.

TIP

Combining Two Paragraphs into One
To combine two paragraphs into one, put the insertion point at the very start of the second paragraph and then press the **Backspace** key on your keyboard.

TIP

Displaying Your Paragraph Marks
To see all the *paragraph breaks* (and other invisible formatting marks) in your page, click the **Show All** button on the Standard toolbar while in Design view.

Typing Symbols and Special Characters

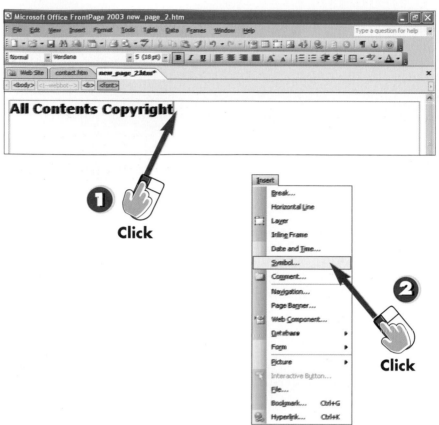

Click

Click

1 Using the mouse pointer, point to the spot in the text where you want to insert the character, and click to position the insertion point there.

2 Open the **Insert** menu and choose **Symbol**.

Sometimes you'll need to insert characters that don't appear on your keyboard, such as the copyright symbol or the accented characters used in languages other than English. For such occasions, FrontPage offers its Symbol dialog box.

Symbols Might Not Display Correctly in Every Browser
The codes FrontPage uses for some symbols work great when the page is viewed through a Windows browser but might not look right when viewed on another computer type (such as a Macintosh). To make your page look great to the non-Windows crowd online, avoid the Symbols dialog box and see a more advanced book to learn to use character codes in HTML.

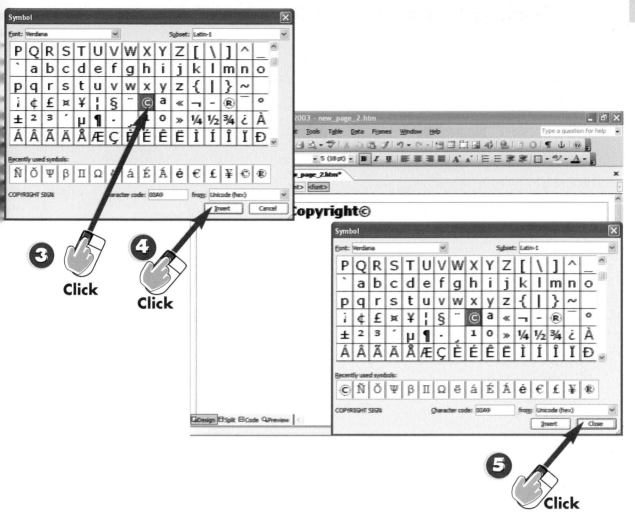

3 Click

4 Click

5 Click

3 The Symbol dialog box opens. Click the symbol you want to insert. The symbol appears next to the **Insert** button.

4 Click the **Insert** button to insert the symbol.

5 The symbol is inserted. Click the **Close** button in the Symbol dialog box to close it.

End

Deleting a Symbol
You delete a symbol exactly as you would delete any other text. See "Replacing (or Deleting) Existing Text" later in this part for help.

Watch Symbols When Changing Fonts
If you change the font (as you learn to do in Part 4) of text containing symbols, recheck the symbols carefully, and redo them if necessary. Sometimes changing fonts messes up symbols.

Selecting Text

Start

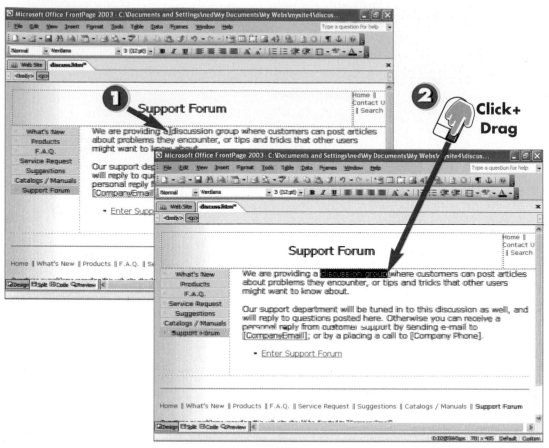

Click + Drag

1 Point to the beginning of the text you want to select.

2 Click and drag to select the desired text. Drag to the right to select all or part of a line; drag up or down to select multiple lines.

End

To perform most activities involving text—such as changing the style of text, deleting text, or replacing text with different text—you must first select (highlight) the text you want to work on. You select text in FrontPage in the same way you select text in most other Windows programs.

Deselecting Text
To deselect text (remove the highlighting), point anywhere in the page and click.

Typing Replaces the Selection
Anything you type automatically replaces any selected text. Even if you type only one character, that character replaces all the selected text. The new text is usually formatted the same way as the text it replaces.

Replacing (or Deleting) Existing Text

Start

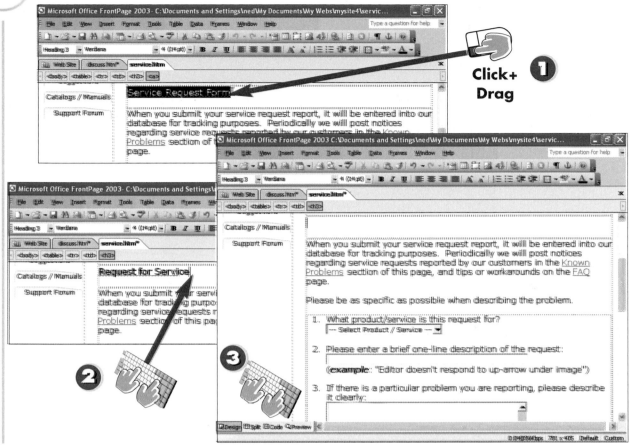

Click+ Drag ❶

❶ Select the text you want to change.

❷ To replace the selected text with new text, type your new text.

❸ To delete the selected text, press the **Delete** key on your keyboard.

End

INTRODUCTION

If you started your page with a template (see Part 2, "Creating New Web Pages"), you've probably got a lot of sample text in your page that you need to replace with your own (or just delete). Even if you didn't use a template to create your page, replacing and deleting text is an essential page-editing skill—and an easy one.

TIP

Replace Text, Keep the Formatting
To replace text with new text formatted the same way—same font, size, and so on (see Part 4)—replace that text (step 2) rather than delete it (step 3). If you delete and then type new text, the new text might not show the same formatting as what you deleted.

Copying Text

Start

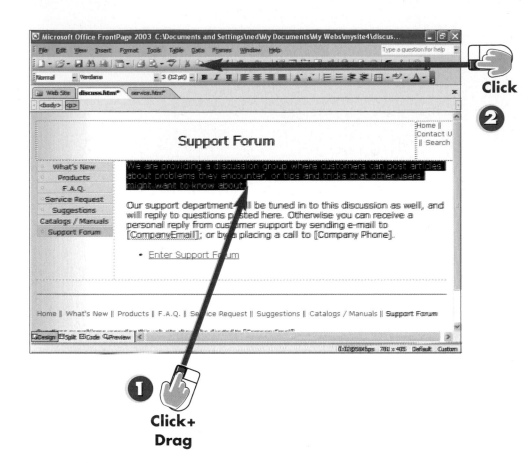

Click

2

1

**Click+
Drag**

1 Select the text you want to copy.

2 Click the **Copy** button on the Standard toolbar.

If you have a block of text you want to use in more than one place on your page, you needn't type it over and over. You can simply type it once and then copy it wherever you need it.

TIP

Copying from Other Programs
To copy text from another Windows program—such as your word processor—to a page, perform steps 1 and 2 in the other program, switch to FrontPage, and perform steps 3 and 4 in the page.

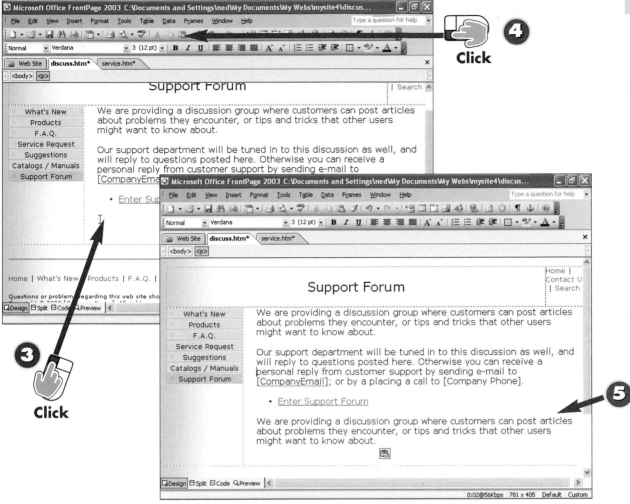

Click

Click

3. Point to the spot where you want to paste the copied text, and click to position the insertion point there.

4. Click the **Paste** button on the Standard toolbar.

5. The copied text is pasted in the spot you specified.

End

Copy As Many Times As You Want!
After step 4, you can move ahead to other editing activities, or you can copy the same text you selected in step 1 again—as many times as you want—by repeating steps 3 and 4 for each copy you want to make.

Moving Text

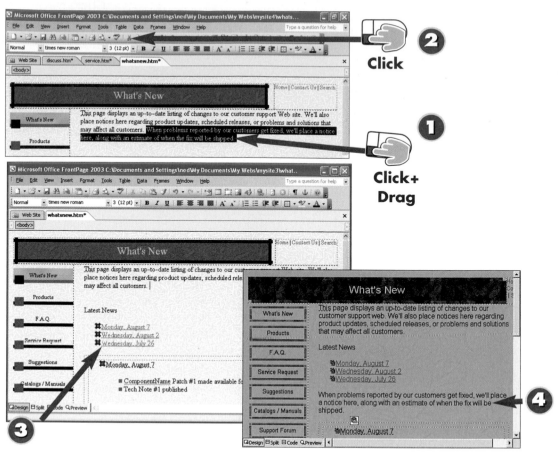

Start

Click ➋

Click+ Drag ➊

➊ Select the text you want to move.

➋ Click the **Cut** button on the Standard toolbar.

➌ Point to the spot where you want to paste the cut text, click to position the insertion point there, and then click the **Paste** button on the Standard toolbar.

➍ The cut text is pasted in the spot you specified.

End

Moving text is like copying—except that you don't leave the original text behind. You *cut* it from one place and then *copy* it in another.

Delete Is Not the Same As Cut

Don't try to use the Delete key on your keyboard instead of clicking the Cut button in step 2 to cut text. Although deleting text removes the text just like issuing a Cut command does, it doesn't remember the text so that it can be pasted in step 3.

Checking Spelling As You Work

Start

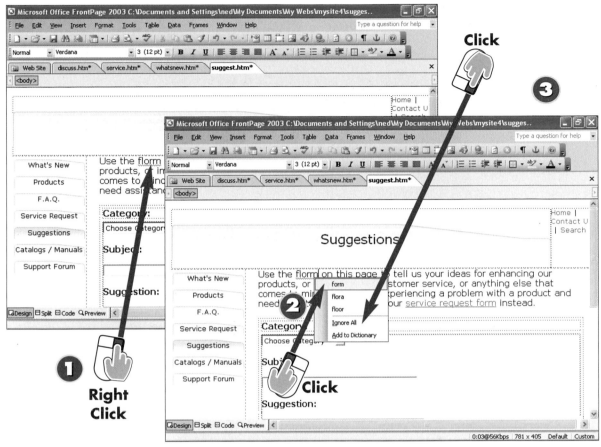

Click

3

1
Right Click

2

Click

1 Right-click the underlined word.

2 Read any suggestions offered in bold atop the shortcut menu. If one is correct, click it to replace the underlined word with the suggestion.

3 If your original word is correct as is, click **Ignore All** to prevent that word from being marked as an error anywhere in the page.

End

While typing in Design view, you might have noticed a zigzag underline. That's the automatic spell-checker at work—it zigzag-underlines any word it doesn't recognize, to alert you to check that word. You can simply fix the word or ignore the underlines when you disagree with the spell-checker.

TIP

The Spell-Checker Can't Catch All Mistakes

The spell-checker marks all words it doesn't recognize. The words might be misspelled, or they might just be names or other words that aren't in FrontPage's dictionary. To add an often-used word (such as your name) to the dictionary so that the checker knows it's not an error, right-click the underlined word and choose **Add to Dictionary** from the shortcut menu that appears.

Running the Spell-Checker

Start

Click

Click

1. With the page whose spelling you want to check displayed onscreen, click the **Spelling** button on the Standard toolbar.

2. The Spelling dialog box opens. Unrecognized words are found in the **Not in Dictionary** box and suggested alternative spellings in the **Suggestions** box.

3. If the word in the Not in Dictionary box is, in fact, correctly spelled, click the **Ignore** button.

Despite the as-you-go spell-checker (see "Checking Spelling As You Work" earlier in this part), it's smart to run FrontPage's on-demand spell-checker, too. If a page is heavily formatted or has small text, the zigzag lines marking your goofs are easy to miss.

Ignore All
When performing step 3, you can click **Ignore All** to make the spell-checker automatically ignore that word everywhere it finds it in this spell-check run.

Adding to the Dictionary
To add an often-used word (such as your name) to the dictionary so that the checker knows it's not an error, click the **Add** button the next time the checker stops on that word.

Click

4

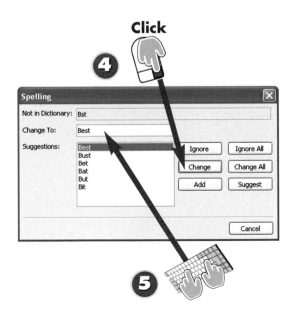

Spelling

Not in Dictionary: Bst

Change To: Best

Suggestions: Best, Bust, Bet, Bat, But, Bit

Ignore | Ignore All
Change | Change All
Add | Suggest

Cancel

5

Microsoft Office FrontPage

The spelling check is complete.

OK

6

Click

4 If the word is misspelled but one suggestion in the Suggestions box is correct, click the suggested word and then click the **Change** button.

5 If the word is misspelled and no correct suggestion appears, type the correct spelling in the **Change To** box and then click the **Change** button.

6 After you perform step 3, 4, or 5, the spell-checker moves through all unrecognized words. After the checker reports that it's finished; click **OK**.

End

Fix a Mistake Everywhere, Automatically
When performing step 4 or 5, you can click **Change All** to make the spell-checker automatically fix that same error (with the same solution) everywhere it finds it in this spell-check run.

Looking Up Synonyms

Start

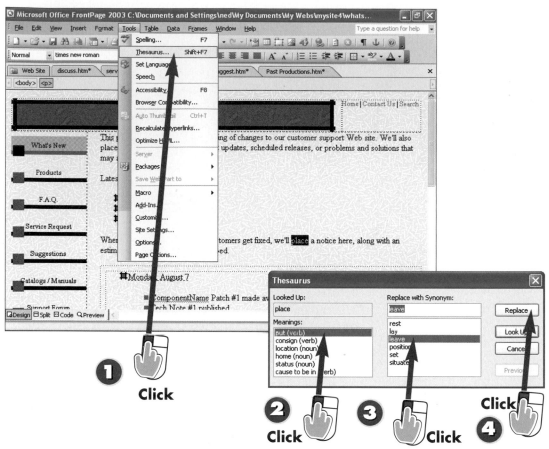

Click

Click **1**

Click **2**

Click **3**

Click **4**

1 After you select the word for which you want to see synonyms, open the **Tools** menu and choose **Thesaurus**.

2 The Thesaurus dialog box opens. If two or more choices are in the **Meanings** list, click the one that most closely matches the meaning you want.

3 In the **Replace with Synonym** list, click the word you want to use.

4 Click the **Replace** button to close the thesaurus and replace your original word with the synonym.

End

Another feature of FrontPage is the built-in thesaurus that can suggest some *synonyms*, alternative words with the same meaning, for text that you've typed.

Canceling the Thesaurus
If you don't like any of the suggested synonyms better than your original word, click **Cancel** in the Thesaurus dialog box to close it.

Finding More Choices
To display a new list of synonyms based on one of the suggestions in the Replace with Synonym list, click the suggestion and then click the **Look Up** button.

Finding Text

Start

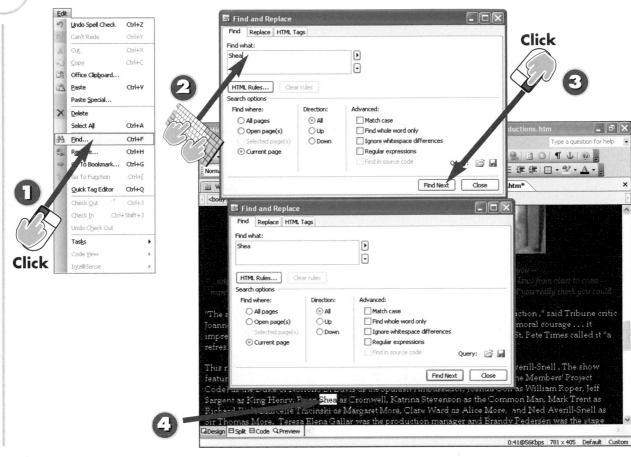

Click

Click

1. After you click at the top of the page containing the text you want to find, open the **Edit** menu and choose **Find**.

2. The Find and Replace dialog box opens with the Find tab displayed. In the **Find what** box, type the word or phrase you want to locate.

3. Click the **Find Next** button. FrontPage locates the first instance of the **Find what** text in the page and selects it.

4. If the instance is the one you wanted to work on, click the **Close** button in the Find and Replace dialog box. If not, click **Find Next** again to move to the next instance.

End

INTRODUCTION

In a long page or site, you might have trouble quickly locating specific words or passages you want to edit or review. That's when FrontPage's Find feature comes in handy.

TIP

Finding By Case
To find only instances of the **Find what** text that match the exact capitalization you typed, click the **Match case** check box in the Advanced area of the Find and Replace dialog box to put a check mark there.

Finding and Replacing Text

Start

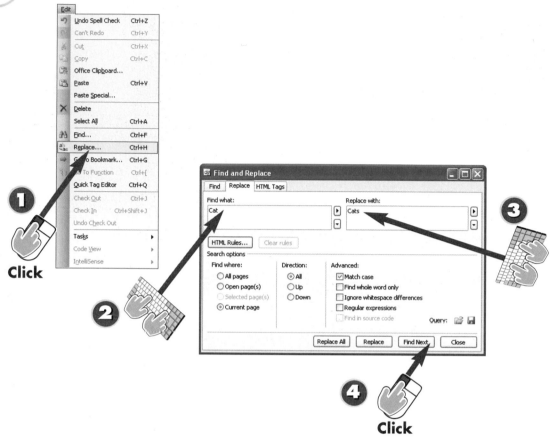

Click

Click

1. After you click at the very top of the page containing the text you want to replace, open the **Edit** menu and choose **Replace**.

2. The Find and Replace dialog box opens with the Replace tab displayed. In the **Find what** box, type the word or phrase you want to change.

3. In the **Replace with** box, type what you want the text from step 2 changed to.

4. To choose which instances of the **Find what** text to change, click the **Find Next** button.

There might be times when you not only need to find text in a Web page, you also have to replace it with something else. That's when FrontPage's Find and Replace feature comes in handy.

Replacing By Case

To change only instances of the **Find what** text that match the exact capitalization you typed, click the **Match case** check box in the Advanced area of the Find and Replace dialog box to put a check mark there.

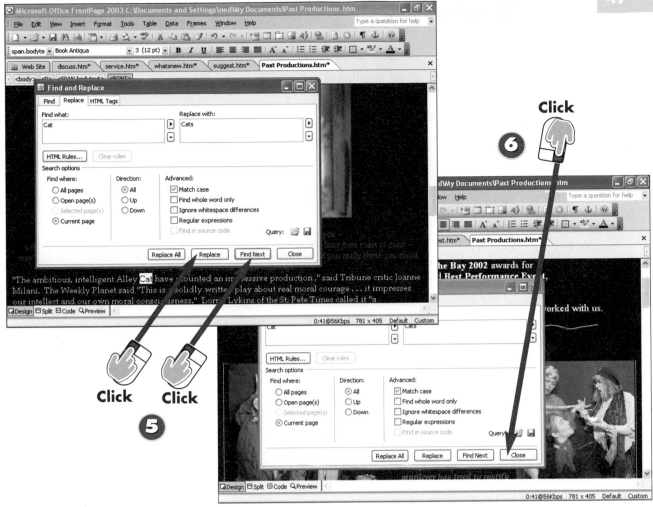

Click

Click **Click**

5

6

5 FrontPage locates the first instance of the text in the page and selects it. To replace it, click the **Replace** button. Click **Find Next** to skip it and find the next instance.

6 FrontPage selects the next instance of the text in the page. Again, click **Replace** or **Find Next**; repeat until all instances of the word have been handled.

End

Making Global Text Changes

To perform a global change—that is, to change all instances of the **Find what** text to the Replace with text without checking each one—click the **Replace All** button in the Find and Replace dialog box.

Dressing Up Your Text

From changing the size and color of text, to adding common emphasis effects such as bolding and italics, you can do a lot with text in FrontPage. Depending on how you approach your page, you might need all—or none—of the text-formatting techniques in this part. For example, if you use a template to create your Web page and just replace the text that's there, the text is preformatted, and you can leave the formatting alone if you're happy with it. In addition, if you choose a theme, you'll find that you can do most or all of your text formatting simply by selecting a *style* (see "Choosing the Style of a Paragraph" later in this part) for each paragraph.

But as your confidence grows, you'll probably want ever-increasing control of text formatting so that you can tune and tailor the look of your text to your precise requirements. In this part, you'll explore all the ways you can change the look of text—from the simple to the sublime.

Tools for Dressing Up Your Text

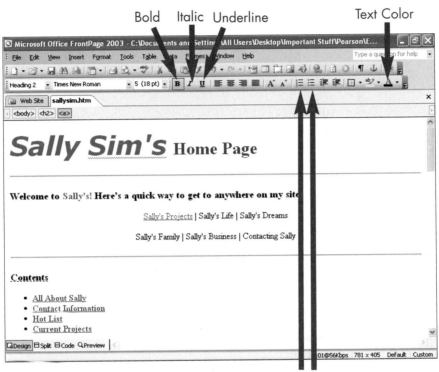

Choosing the Style of a Paragraph

Start

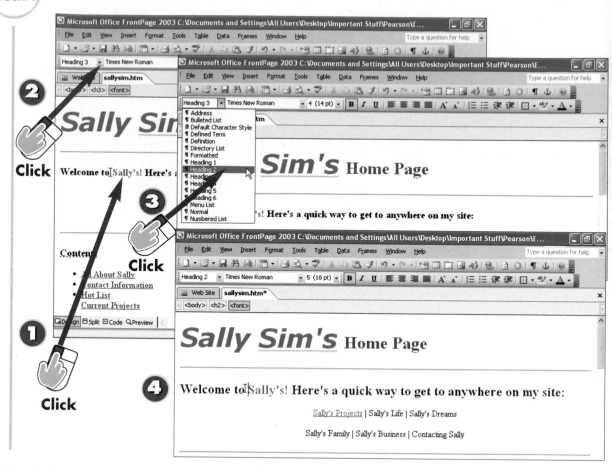

Click

Click

Click

1 In Design view, click anywhere within the paragraph you want to format. (You do not need to select the paragraph.)

2 Click the **down arrow** on the right end of the **Style** box on the Formatting toolbar to open the Style list.

3 In the Style list, click the name of the style you want to apply.

4 The style is applied to the selected text.

End

The most important step in controlling the appearance of text is choosing the text's *paragraph style* from the Style list. There are many styles to choose from, but the most important are the six different Heading styles (from big Heading 1 to little Heading 6), Normal style (for ordinary, everyday paragraphs), and the List styles (see the task "Creating a Simple List" later in this part).

TIP

Changing the Style of Multiple Paragraphs
To apply a style to multiple, consecutive paragraphs all at once, click anywhere in the first paragraph and drag down through the paragraphs to anywhere in the last paragraph. Then choose your style.

Indenting a Paragraph

Start

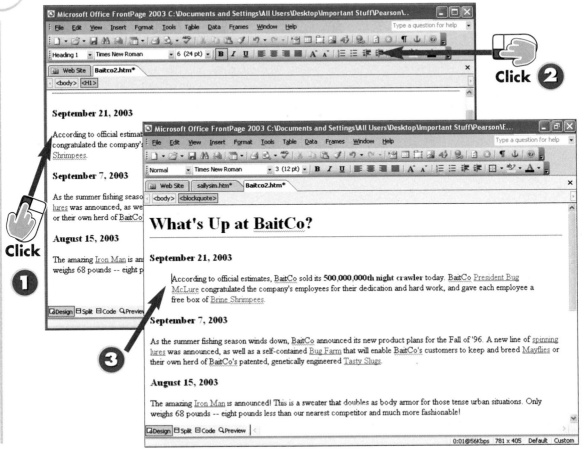

Click ❷

Click ❶

❸

End

❶ Click anywhere within the paragraph you want to indent. (You do not need to select the paragraph.)

❷ Click the **Increase Indent** button on the Formatting toolbar. (To indent farther, click the **Increase Indent** button multiple times.)

❸ The paragraph is indented.

INTRODUCTION

To *indent* a paragraph is to push it inward from the margin to make it stand out on the page and to better show that the indented text is a part of the heading or other text above it. Indenting selected paragraphs can give your page structure and visual variety.

TIP

Indenting Multiple Paragraphs
To indent multiple, consecutive paragraphs at once, click anywhere in the first paragraph and drag down through the paragraphs to anywhere in the last paragraph. Then click the **Increase Indent** button.

TIP

Removing Indents
To remove the indent, click anywhere in the indented paragraph, and then click the **Decrease Indent** button on the Formatting toolbar.

Aligning Paragraphs on the Left, Right, or in the Center

Start

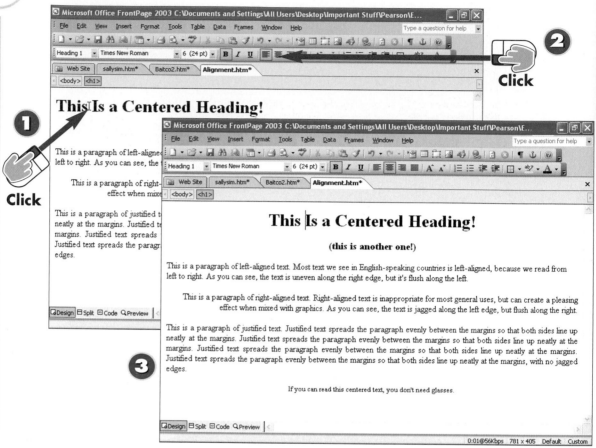

1 Click anywhere within the paragraph you want to align. (You do not need to select the paragraph.)

2 Click one of the four alignment buttons on the Formatting toolbar: **Align Left**, **Center**, **Align Right**, or **Justify**.

3 The paragraph is aligned (here, center-aligned).

End

You can align any paragraph in any of four different ways: tight up against the left side of the page (left alignment), centered on the page (center alignment), hard up to the right side of the page (right alignment), or justified (spread evenly from margin to margin, like a newspaper column).

TIP

Aligning Multiple Paragraphs

To align multiple, consecutive paragraphs, click anywhere in the first paragraph and drag down through the paragraphs to anywhere in the last paragraph. Then click the alignment button you want.

Making Text Bold, Italic, or Underlined

Start

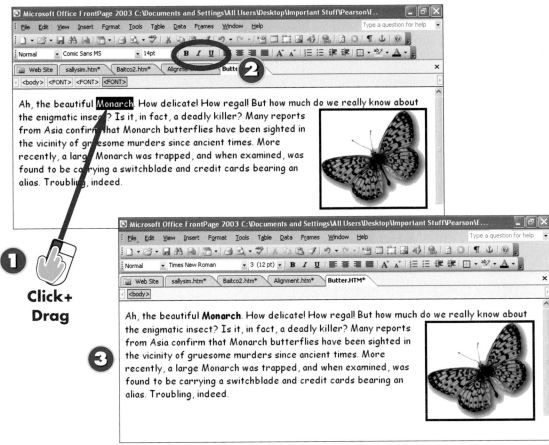

Click + Drag

1. Select the exact characters you want to format.

2. Click the **Bold** button, **Italic** button, or **Underline** button to format the selected characters.

3. The text effect is applied to the selected text (in this example, the text is made bold).

End

INTRODUCTION

Just as in any letter or report you might create, **bold**, *italic*, and underlining are valuable tools in a Web page for making text stand out or for making it match editorial standards (such as setting book titles in italics). They're easy to use, but use them sparingly; too much of this stuff makes text busy and hard to read.

Removing Bold, Italic, or Underlining

To remove bold, italic, or underlining, select the text and click the button again. For example, to de-bold some bold text, select the text and click the **Bold** button.

Choosing a Font for Text

Start

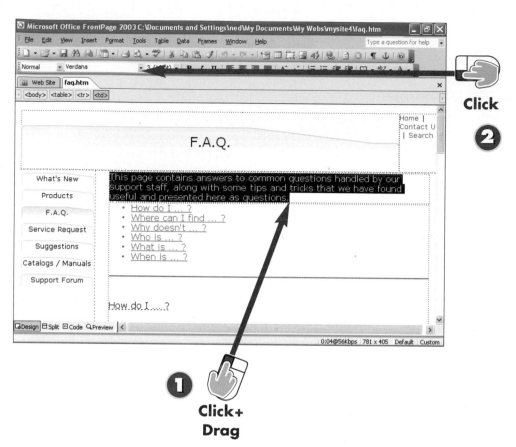

Click

2

1

**Click+
Drag**

1 Select the exact characters to which you want to apply a new font.

2 Click the **down arrow** to the right of the **Font** box in the Formatting toolbar to open the Font list.

The best way to control the appearance of text is to choose an appropriate style ("Choosing the Style of a Paragraph" earlier in this part), especially if you use a theme. But beyond styles, you can dress up text even more by choosing a particular typeface—or *font*—for it.

Character Formatting Changes *Only* What You Select

Fonts are a form of character formatting, not paragraph formatting, so they affect only the exact characters you select. To apply a font to a whole paragraph, you must select the whole paragraph. The same is true of other character formatting, such as size, bold, italic, underlining, and color.

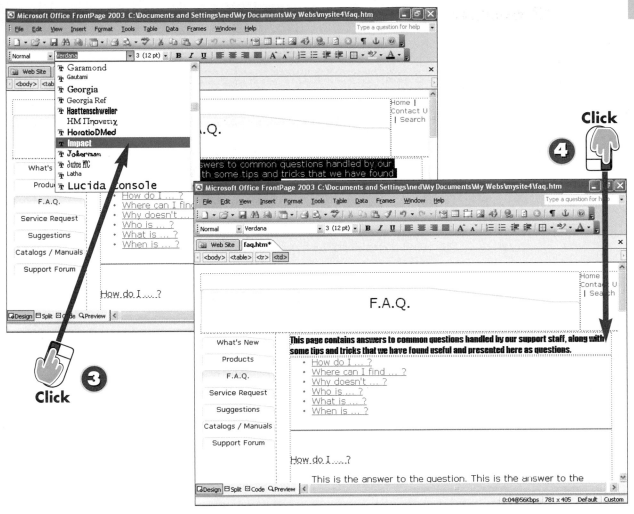

3 Click the font you want to apply.

4 The font you chose is applied to the selected text. Click anywhere in your page to deselect the text.

Not All Browsers Support Your Font Choices
Some browsers (especially unusual or older ones) don't support fonts, although nearly all browsers support a standard list of basic fonts that includes Times New Roman, Arial, and Courier. If you've used fonts, visitors using those browsers will still see your text, but they might not see it styled exactly the way you intend.

Making Text Bigger or Smaller

Start

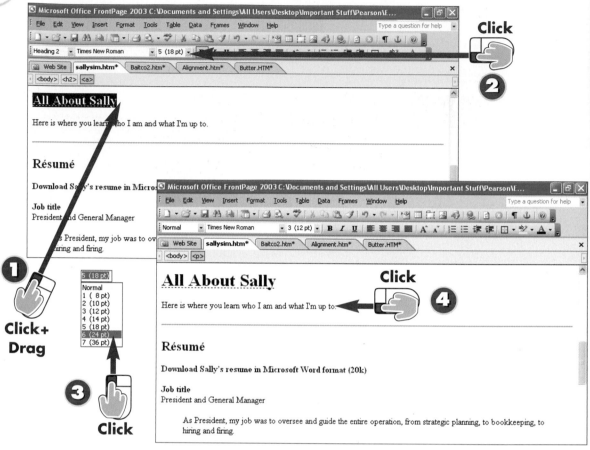

1 Select the exact characters you want to make bigger or smaller.

2 Click the down arrow to the right of the **Font Size** box in the Formatting toolbar to open the Font Size list.

3 Choose a size, from 1 (smallest) to 36 (largest). Alternatively, choose **Normal** to allow the applied paragraph style to determine the font size.

4 The selected font is resized. Click anywhere in your page to deselect the text.

End

The paragraph style you choose determines the size of the text within that paragraph. For example, if text set in Heading 3 style looks too small to you, change it to a bigger style, such as Heading 2 or Heading 1. You can fine-tune the size of selected text easily when the size chosen by the style isn't exactly what you want.

TIP

"Point" Sizes Are a Little Arbitrary

Next to each size in the Font Size list is a point size (8 pt., 10 pt., and so on). In publishing, *points* measure the height of capital letters (72 pt. = 1 inch). The points are shown to help you estimate the size, but they're not particularly meaningful, because the exact size of text depends on the screen dimensions of the computer monitor on which it is viewed.

Choosing the Color of Text

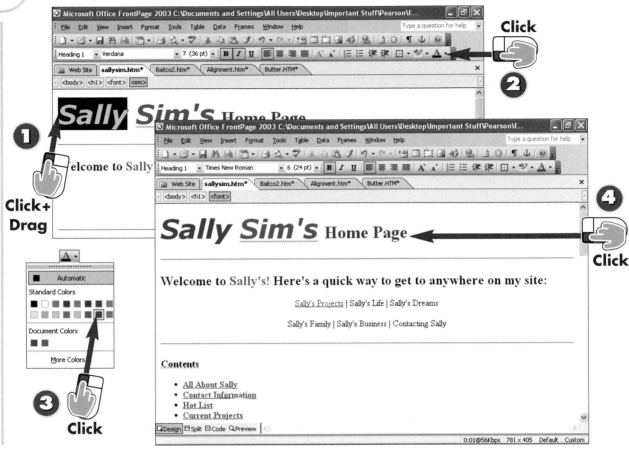

1. Select the exact characters for which you want to choose a color.

2. If the color shown in the **Font Color** button is what you want, click the button to apply the color. For a different color, click the **down arrow** on the **Font Color** button.

3. Click the colored square containing the color you want to apply. (To allow the paragraph style to determine the color, click **Automatic**.)

4. The color is applied to the selected text. Click anywhere in your page to deselect the text.

INTRODUCTION

If you choose a theme or create your page using a template, text colors have already been selected to go well with one another and to contrast properly with any colored background. So you might never need to choose text colors. Still, you might find yourself wanting to give a heading or other selected text its own unique color.

More Color Options
If you don't like any of the colors in the box that drops down from the Font Color button, click **More Colors**. A palette appears, showing hundreds of color choices. Click a color and then click **OK**.

Browsers Can Trump Your Colors
Users can configure their browsers to reject "custom" text and background colors. Users who do this will not see the text colors you choose, but will see the text itself just fine.

Giving Text a "Highlight" Color

Start

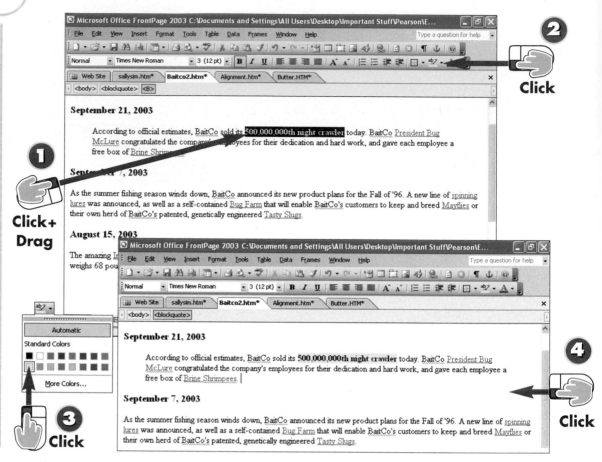

Click+ Drag

Click

Click

Click

1. Select the exact characters you want to highlight.

2. If the color shown in the **Highlight Color** button is what you want, click the button to apply the color. For a different color, click the **down arrow** on the **Highlight Color** button.

3. Click the colored square containing the color you want to apply. (To allow the paragraph style to determine the color, click **Automatic**.)

4. The highlight color is applied to the selected text. Click anywhere in your page to deselect the text.

End

A *highlight color* lays a bar of transparent color over selected text, creating the same effect you get when you mark printed text with a highlight marker. Used sparingly, a highlight color is a fun and effective way to make text stand out.

TIP

Expanded Choices for Highlight Colors
If you don't like any of the colors in the box that drops down from the Highlight Color button, click **More Colors**. A palette appears, showing hundreds of color choices. Click a color and then click **OK**.

HINT

Keep Your Text Legible
When choosing font colors, highlight colors, and a background (see Part 6, "Adding and Formatting Pictures"), be careful that all the colors contrast well enough to make the text readable.

"Painting" the Formatting

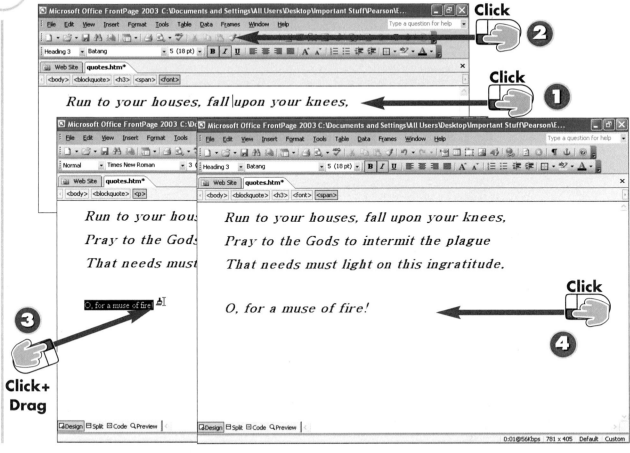

1 Click in the paragraph whose formatting you want to copy.

2 Click the **Format Painter** button on the Standard toolbar. (When you move your pointer onto the work area, it becomes a paintbrush to show it is active.)

3 Select the entire paragraph to which you want to apply the formatting.

4 The formatting is applied. Click anywhere in the page to deselect the paragraph.

Suppose that you have two paragraphs that you want formatted the same. FrontPage features a *Format Painter* that lets you easily copy all paragraph formatting (style, alignment, indent) and character formatting (font, size, color, bold, and so on) from one paragraph to another so that the two paragraphs are formatted identically.

Painting Just Characters

To copy a character formatting (without any paragraph formatting), select some text formatted the way you want (but not a whole paragraph), click the **Format Painter** button, and then select the exact characters to which you want the character formatting applied.

Finding the Advanced Text-Formatting Options

Start

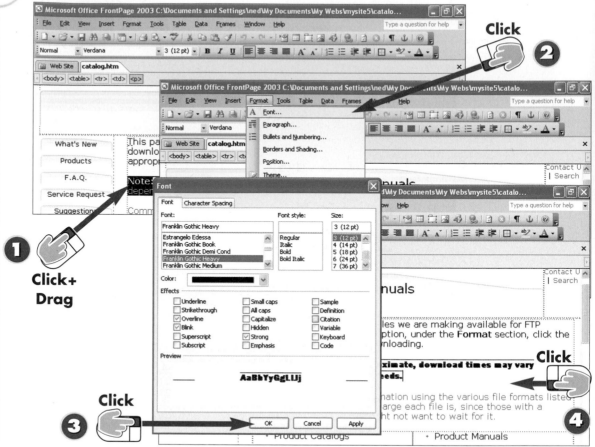

Click

2

Click+ Drag

1

Click

3

Click

4

1 Select the exact characters you want to format.

2 Open the **Format** menu and choose **Font**.

3 Choose from the lists and check the check boxes on the tab. When the **Preview** area shows the formatting you want, click **OK**.

4 The formatting is applied. Click anywhere in the page to deselect the characters.

End

INTRODUCTION

The use of most other, more advanced formatting options—such as strikethrough, superscript/subscript, and small caps—can make your page too busy and hard to read, and they're not supported in some browsers. But just in case you feel ambitious, here's how to apply a variety of different advanced formatting options.

TIP

Changing Character Spacing

To change the spacing between characters in selected text, complete steps 1 and 2 in this task to open the Font dialog box, click the **Character Spacing** tab, and select from the options offered there.

Creating a Simple List

Start

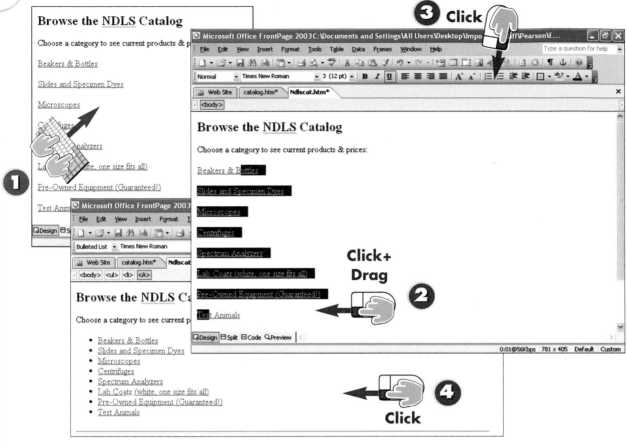

③ **Click**

Click+ Drag ②

④ **Click**

① Type the list items, pressing **Enter** after each so that each list item is its own paragraph.

② Select the entire list by clicking anywhere in the top item, holding down the mouse button, and dragging to anywhere in the last item.

③ Click the **Numbering** or **Bullets** button on the Formatting toolbar.

④ The selected text is formatted as a list (in this example, a bulleted list). Click anywhere in the page to deselect the characters.

End

Changing the Bullet or Numbering Style of a List

Start

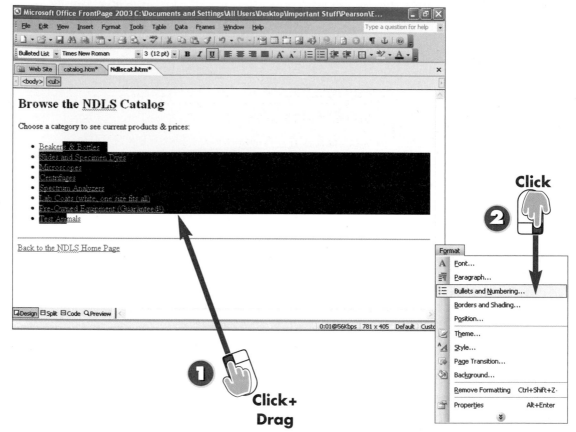

Click+ Drag

Click

1 Select the list by clicking anywhere in the top item, holding down the mouse button, and dragging to anywhere in the last item.

2 Open the **Format** menu and choose **Bullets and Numbering**.

You can make a good-looking list just by clicking a button, as you did in the previous task. But you don't have to settle for what you get. You can easily modify the appearance of a list, choosing the numbering style (A, B, C; I, II, III; and so on) or bullet symbol.

Changing Bullets in a Theme

TIP

If your page has a theme, the theme might put cool, graphical bullets on your bulleted lists, and you won't see the bullet options shown in this task. Instead, you'll get a different tab on which you can click a **Browse** button to replace the bullets with another bullet-size image of your choice.

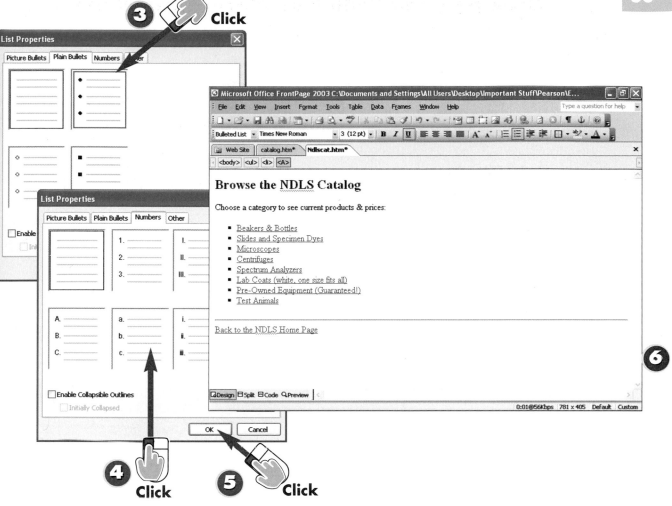

Click

Click **Click**

③ The List Properties dialog box opens. To choose a bullet style, click the **Plain Bullets** tab, and click the box showing the type of bullets you want.

④ To choose a number (or consecutive letters) style, choose the **Numbers** tab, and click the box showing the type of numbering you want.

⑤ Click **OK** to close the List Properties dialog box.

⑥ The selected text is formatted using the bullet or number scheme you selected. Click anywhere in the page to deselect the characters.

End

More List Options
On the Other tab of the List Properties dialog box, you can choose from a few kinds of lists other than bulleted and numbered. These aren't used often, so I won't show them here—but if you're curious, try them out.

Nesting Items in a List

Start

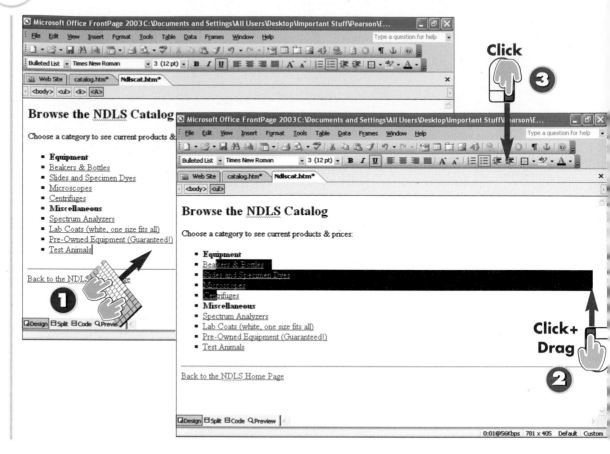

Click

Click+ Drag

1 Create the list as a simple, unnested list. (Do not indent any items yet.)

2 Select a group of items to be nested.

3 Click the **Increase Indent** button on the Formatting toolbar twice.

INTRODUCTION

A complex, or *nested*, list contains some items indented under others. This book's Table of Contents is an example; the tasks are nested beneath each part heading. You can create such lists on your Web pages, going several levels deep and even changing the bullet or number style for nested objects to help them stand out.

HINT

Bullet Styles in a Nested List
Besides varying the number style for each level in a numbered list, you can also dress up a bulleted list by varying the bullet style with each level.

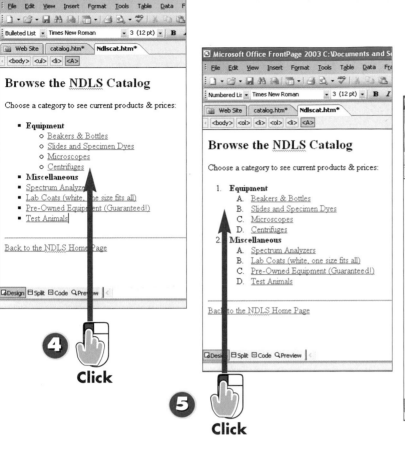

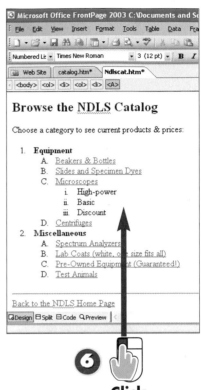

4 The selected text is indented, or nested. Click anywhere in the page to deselect the text.

5 To change the bullet or number style for the nested items, select them and then choose a style as described earlier in "Changing the Bullet or Numbering Style of a List."

6 To create each deeper level of nesting, select the items to be moved to the next level, and click **Increase Indent** twice.

End

Changing Where Numbering Begins

In a numbered list, the numbers in each nested portion are numbered independently, starting at 1 (or a, or I, and so on). That's the way outlines and other nested lists are usually structured. If you want to change where the numbering begins in any part of the list, select that part, open the **Format** menu, and choose **Bullets and Numbering**; then choose your desired starting number under **Start At**.

Creating a Collapsible List

Start

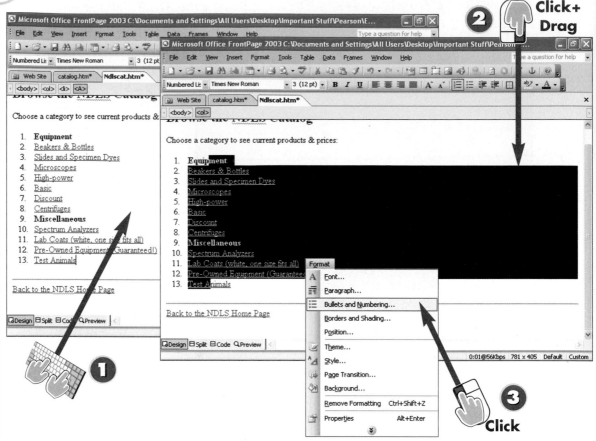

② Click+ Drag

③ Click

① Create a simple list, pressing **Enter** after each so that each list item is its own paragraph. (Don't nest anything yet.)

② Select the list by clicking in the top item, holding down the mouse button, and dragging to anywhere in the last item.

③ Open the **Format** menu and choose **Bullets and Numbering**.

④ The Bullets and Numbering dialog box opens. Click the **Enable Collapsible Outlines** check box to place a check mark there.

INTRODUCTION

A really long list is a problem in a Web page; it forces the visitor to scroll too much, and it makes finding headings in the list difficult because of all the nested detail. The answer is a *collapsible list*, a nested list in which only top-level items show—at first. When the visitor clicks any top-level item, all nested items beneath it appear.

TIP

Tell Visitors the List Is Collapsible
Some folks on the Web need a little coaching on collapsible lists. Near the list, it's usually a good idea to add "Click any item to see more detailed choices," or words to that effect.

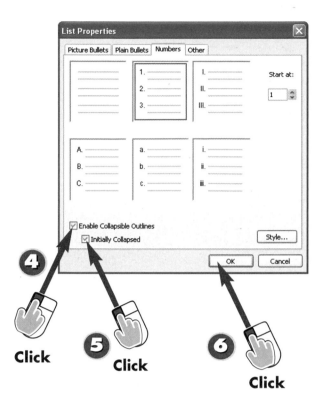

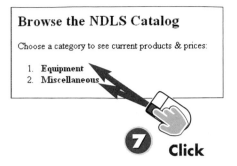

7 **Click**

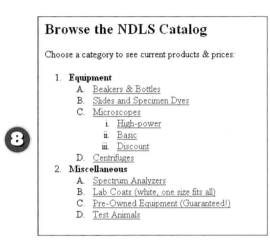

8

Click

4

5 **Click**

Click

6 **Click**

---

5 Click the **Initially Collapsed** check box to place a check mark there. That way, the nested items will be hidden when the visitor arrives at the page.

6 Click **OK** to close the List Properties dialog box.

7 Nest items as described in the "Nesting Items in a List" earlier in this part, save the page, and then click a main level item while previewing the page in your Web browser.

8 The nested items are revealed.

TIP

Seeing Your Results
The collapsing effect of a collapsed list does not show up in the Normal tab of FrontPage's Page view. To see your list do its thing, save your page, and then click the **Preview** tab or preview the page in your browser. Clicking a list item displays items nested beneath it; clicking it again hides them.

Making Hyperlinks

You've seen links—they're the things in a Web page that you can click to visit a different page, or to initiate an action such as a file download.

Although in some ways links might seem like one of the more technical aspects of a Web page, they're surprisingly easy to create in FrontPage 2003. The only tricky part is deciding where you want a link to lead; the rest is a piece of cake.

In this part, you'll learn what links are, how they work, and how to link from your pages to other pages on the Internet, to files, and to email addresses. You'll also learn the basics of linking from one of your own pages to another of your own pages—the kind of linking that forms a multipage Web site. (Keep in mind that when you create and manage a FrontPage Web site, you gain access to an array of tools for easily linking all the pages in your Web site. You'll learn about those in Part 9.)

Link-Making Tools

Insert Hyperlink

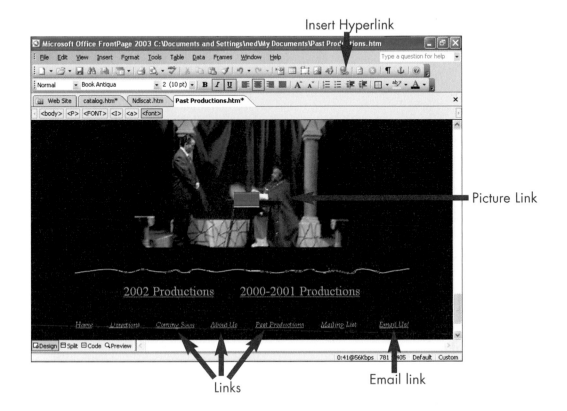

Picture Link

Links

Email link

Exploring How Links Work

Start

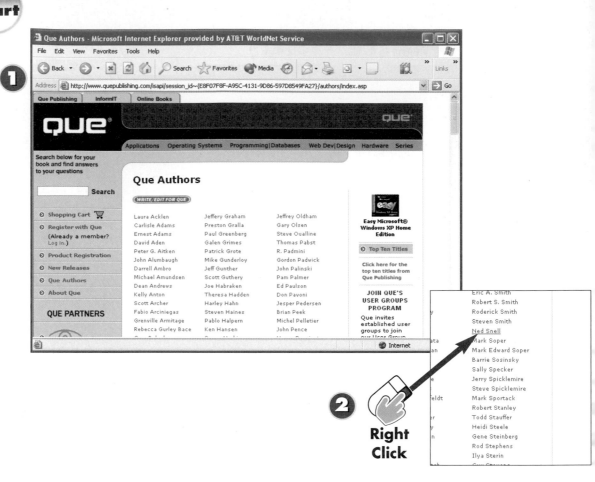

1

2 Right Click

1 After you've opened your Web browser and connected to the Internet, surf to a page you like that contains links.

2 Point to a link whose link source is text, and right-click it.

INTRODUCTION

Every link has two parts: the *link source*—the text, picture, or button that a visitor clicks to activate the link—and the *URL*—the address of the page to which that link takes the visitor. Creating links is really just a matter of creating the link source in your page and then adding the URL behind it.

TIP

Finding Links
When the link source is text, it usually appears underlined and in a unique color. When you point at a link (either text or a picture), the pointer changes from an arrow to a pointing finger.

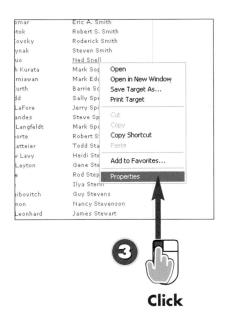

Click

Choose **Properties** from the shortcut menu that appears.

The Properties dialog box opens, noting the address (URL) to which the link points, along with other information.

End

TIP

What About Those Addresses Ending in "ASP"?
Most links point to a file path—for example,
http://myserver.com/index.html. Links ending in **.asp?** tell the server to do some special processing to access the latest information for the page they point to.

Creating Links to Other Web Pages

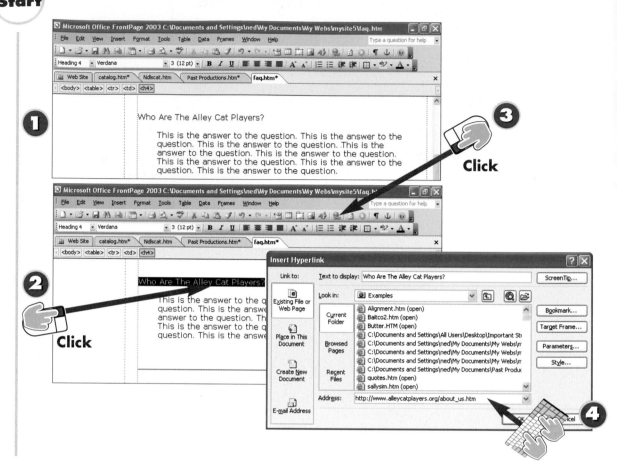

1 In FrontPage, on the page to which you want to add the link, type and format the text that will serve as the link source.

2 Select the text.

3 Click the **Insert Hyperlink** button on the Standard toolbar.

4 If you know the URL of the page to which the link should lead, type it in the **Address** text box (be sure to include the **http://** part) and skip to step 8.

INTRODUCTION

Now that you grasp the basics of what a link is made of, you're ready to create one to another Web page. Whether you know the exact URL of the page you want to link to or you need to surf to the page to find it, creating a link is a snap.

TIP

Pictures Can Be Link Sources, Too
See the task "Using a Picture As a Link" later in this part to learn about using a picture as a link source.

HINT

Keep Link Sources *Short!*
Try to keep the link source short. If the link will be text that's within a paragraph a few lines long, don't highlight the whole paragraph in step 1; just select an appropriate word or two to serve as the link source.

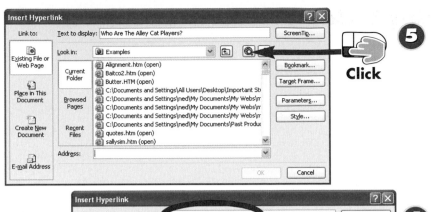

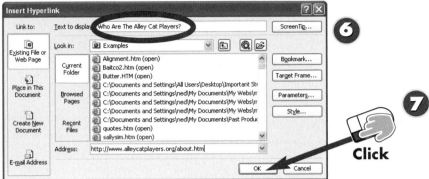

5 If you don't know the address of the page to which you want to link, click the **Browse the Web** button to the right of the **Look in** list. Your Web browser opens.

6 Surf to the page. Then, while viewing the page to which you want to link, press **Alt+Tab** to switch back to the Insert Hyperlink dialog box.

7 Click **OK** in the Insert Hyperlink dialog box to add the link.

8 The link is added. (Use your mouse pointer to point to the link; notice that the pointer changes to a pointing hand.)

End

HINT

You Might Need to Get Online
Depending on the way your PC and Internet software are set up, you might need to connect to the Internet between steps 5 and step 6.

TIP

Avoid Reformatting Link Source Text
After finishing a text link, avoid monkeying with the character formatting of the link source text. Browsers display link source text with unique formatting to help the visitor instantly identify links. You don't want your character formatting to make your links hard for visitors to see.

Linking to Files So Your Visitors Can Download Them

Start

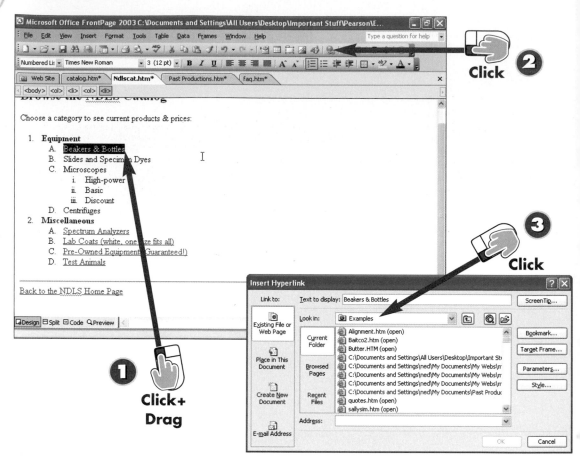

1. After you've prepared the file to which you want to link and created the link source in your Web page, click and drag to select the link source.

2. Click the **Insert Hyperlink** button on the Standard toolbar.

3. The Insert Hyperlink dialog box opens. Navigate to the folder containing the file to which you want to link.

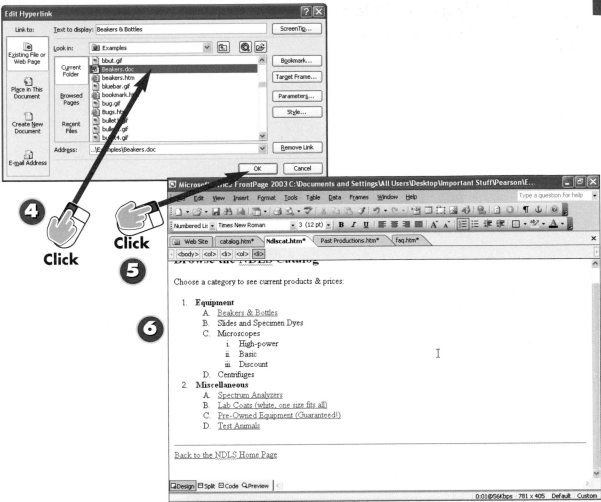

4 Click the file's name to select it.

5 Click **OK**.

6 The link to the file is created.

End

Be Informative
In the link source text (or near it), it's courteous to tell your visitors the file type (so that they can tell whether it's a file they're equipped to view) and size (so they can estimate how long it will take to download at the speed of their Internet connection).

Linking to an Email Address

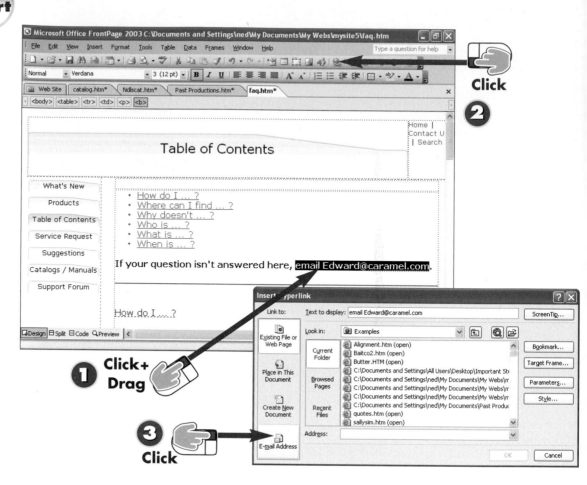

1 Select the text you want to use as the link source for the mailto link.

2 Click the **Insert Hyperlink** button on the Standard toolbar.

3 The Insert Hyperlink dialog box opens. In the Link to bar, click the **E-mail Address** button.

A *signature* tells visitors who created (or manages) the Web page they are viewing. Often, the signature includes a *mailto* link, which points to the email address of the Web page's author. You can create mailto links for signatures, or anywhere you want to help your visitor conveniently send email to you (or whomever).

Forms Help Visitors Contact You

A mailto link isn't the only way your visitors can contact you. You can also provide a response form that enables visitors to send you questions or comments right from the Web page, without opening their email programs.

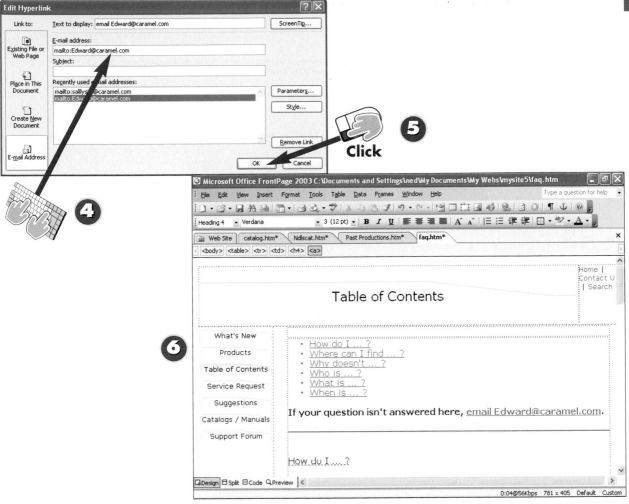

4 Type the email address to which you want to link in the **E-mail address** field.

5 Click **OK**.

6 The link is created.

End

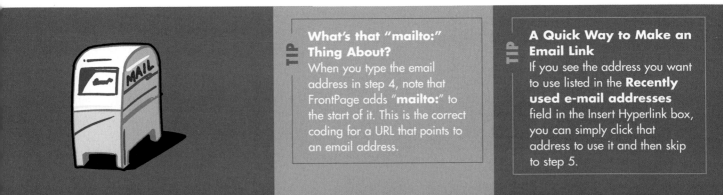

Creating Bookmarks to Link To

Start

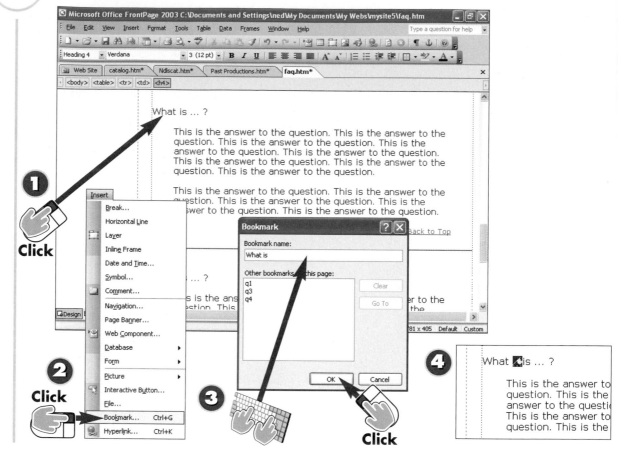

1 Click

2 Click

3 Click

4 Click

1 Click a spot on a Web page where you want a link to lead.

2 Open the **Insert** menu and choose **Bookmark** to insert a bookmark in the spot you chose.

3 The Bookmark dialog box opens. Type a name for the bookmark in the **Bookmark name** field and click **OK**.

4 The bookmark is added in the spot you specified.

End

Linking to a Bookmark

Start

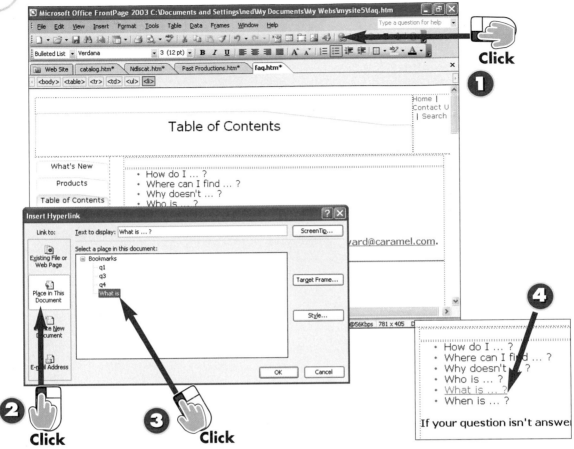

1 Create and select the link source, as you would when creating any kind of link, and then click the **Insert Hyperlink** button.

2 The Insert Hyperlink dialog box opens. In the Link to bar, click **Place in This Document**.

3 In the list of bookmarks that appears, click the name of the bookmark you want this link to lead to, and then click **OK**.

4 The link is created.

End

INTRODUCTION

After you've inserted your bookmarks, you can create links to them as easily as you do to anything else—more easily, actually. Note that you can link from anywhere on a page to bookmarks elsewhere in the same page (as you do in this task), or from one page to bookmarks in another (see Part 9 for more information).

TIP

A Bookmark by Any Other Name...

What FrontPage calls a *bookmark* is often called an *anchor* or a *target* in other Web-authoring programs. And just to make things really confusing, the Netscape Navigator browser calls the shortcuts users create to easily go to Web pages *bookmarks*, as opposed to *favorites*, which is what Internet Explorer calls those shortcuts.

Editing Links

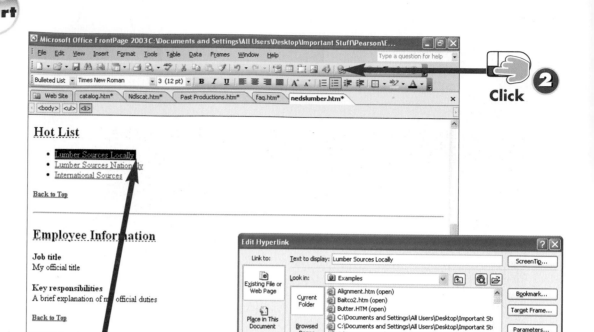

Click

Double-click

Click

1. While viewing the page that contains the link in Design view, double-click the link to select it.

2. Click the **Insert Hyperlink** button.

3. Change anything you want in the Edit Hyperlink dialog box (which is identical to the Insert Hyperlink dialog box, except for its name).

4. Click **OK**.

End

A Fast Way to Link to Oft-Used URLs
In both the Edit Hyperlink and Insert Hyperlink dialog boxes, note that there's a down arrow to the right of the Address field. To link to a URL you've recently used for another link, click the arrow and then choose the URL from the list that appears.

Using a Picture As a Link

Start

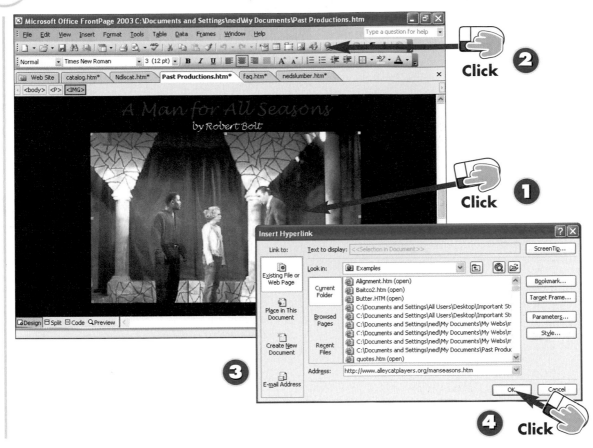

Click ②

Click ①

③

④ **Click**

① Click the picture you want to make into a link to select it.

② Click the **Insert Hyperlink** button on the Standard toolbar.

③ The Insert Hyperlink dialog box opens. Create a link to a URL, a file, an email address, or a bookmark exactly as shown in previous tasks.

④ Click **OK**.

End

Testing Your Links

Start

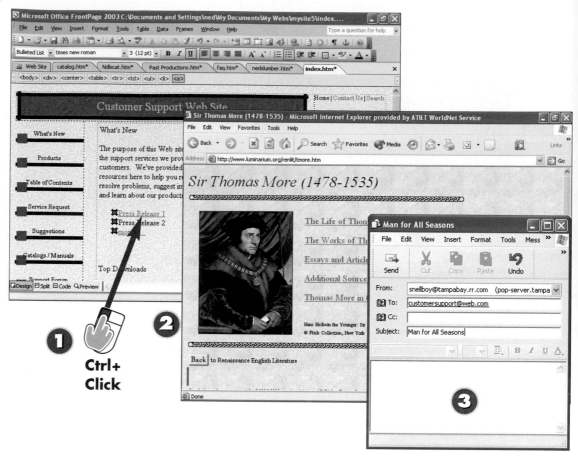

Ctrl+ Click

① ② ③

---

① While viewing your page in Design view, **Ctrl+click** the link you want to test. (Press and hold down the Ctrl key, point to the link, click, and then release the Ctrl key.)

② If the link leads to a Web page, your Web browser will open and display that page.

③ If the link leads to an email address, your email program will open and display a new message window, with the email address already entered.

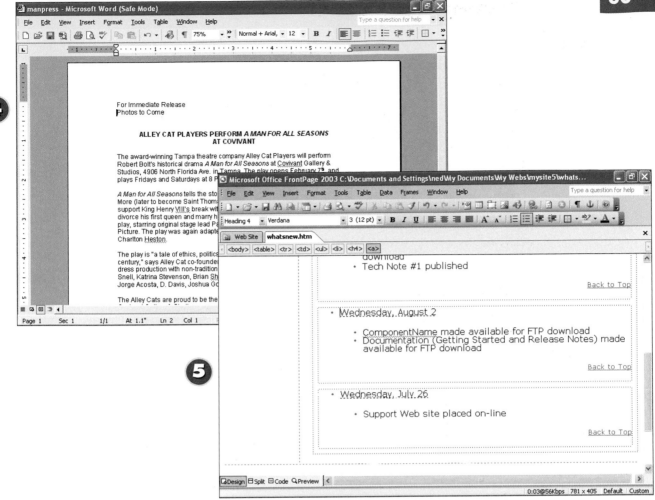

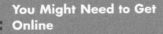

④ If the link leads to a file, Windows opens whatever program it needs to display that file.

⑤ If the link leads to a bookmark, no program opens; FrontPage scrolls to the spot in the Web page where that bookmark appears.

End

TIP

You Might Need to Get Online

Depending on the way your PC and Internet software are set up, you might need to connect to the Internet after step 2 if the link points to a Web page.

Removing Links

Start

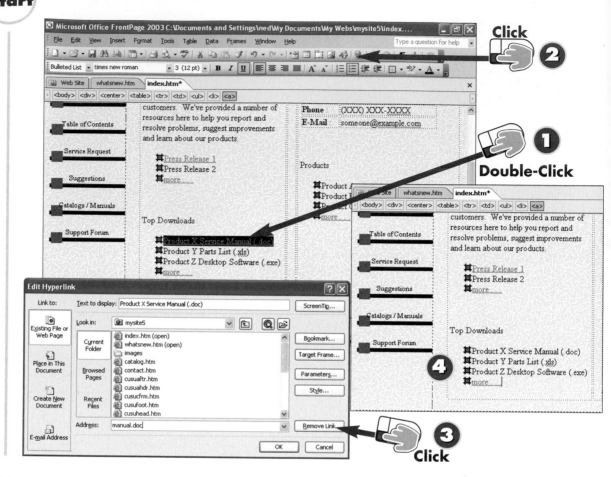

Click ➋

Double-Click ➊

Click ➌

While viewing the page in Design view, double-click the link to select it.

Click the **Insert Hyperlink** button.

Click the **Remove Link** button in the Edit Hyperlink dialog box, and click **OK**.

The text or picture remains but no longer acts as a link.

End

Linking to Your Own Web Pages

Start

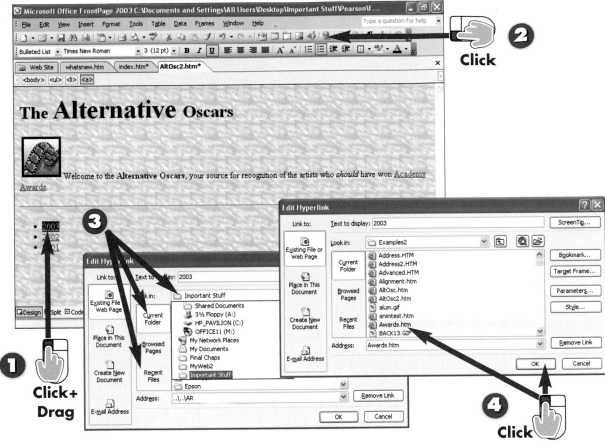

Click

Click+ Drag

Click

1. After you've created both Web pages, open the page in which you will create the link, and select the link source.

2. Click the **Insert Hyperlink** button on the Standard toolbar.

3. Use the **Current Folder** and **Recent Files** buttons, or the **Look in** list and the folders beneath it, to navigate to the folder in which the page you're linking to is stored.

4. In the list of files, click the name of the page to which you're linking and click **OK**. The link is added.

End

The best way to link among your own pages is to build them together as a Web site, as you'll do in Part 9. Doing so lets you easily manage the links, build navigation bars, and do other things that enhance the usability of your site.

TIP

See a Map of Your Links

After creating the link (but with the page containing the link still open in Page view), click the **Hyperlinks** button in the Views bar to see a map of the links in the page and where they lead.

Adding and Formatting Pictures

The pictures and other graphical elements in your pages add not only useful content but also style. Even better, adding pictures is easier than you might think. In this part, you'll learn not only how to add pictures, but also how to make them look great. (Part 7 builds on this part, showing you still more ways to dress up your page with graphics, sound, and motion.)

While adding pictures to your pages, keep in mind that every picture lengthens the time it takes the page to fully materialize on a visitor's screen. You know from your own surfing trips how frustrating a slow Web page is, especially when it's slow just because it has too many pictures. (In Part 12, you'll learn how FrontPage 2003 helps you predict the online performance of your page so that you can fine-tune it before you publish.) In this part and in Part 7, you'll learn to make the choices that will make your pages both beautiful *and* quick.

FrontPage Picture Tools

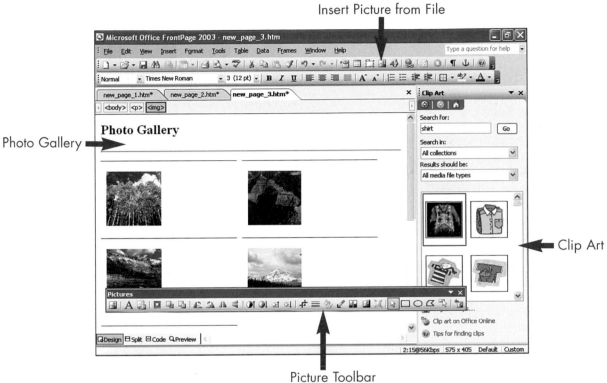

Insert Picture from File

Photo Gallery

Clip Art

Picture Toolbar

Inserting Clip Art

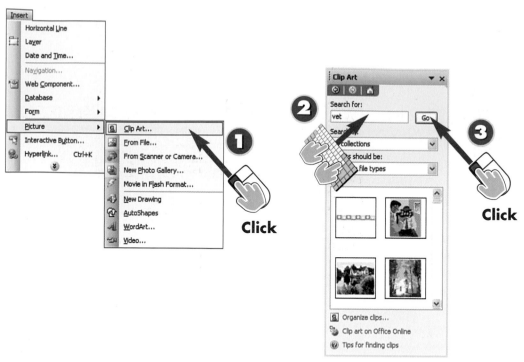

Click

Click

1 Click in your page where you want to insert the clip art and open the **Insert** menu, choose **Picture**, and then choose **Clip Art**.

2 The Clip Art task pane opens. In the **Search box**, type a word or phrase describing the sort of picture you want.

3 Click the **Go** button.

INTRODUCTION

Even if you don't have a specific image you want to add to your page you might use a few pictures to dress it up. Enter Microsoft's built-in Clip Art gallery. The Clip Art gallery lets you quickly add to a page any item from the clip library, which contains thousands of graphics, photos, sound clips, and animations.

TIP

Try Multiple Search Terms
You can type more than one word in the **Search for** text box (for example, "circus clown") to narrow the search even further, but one well-chosen word usually works best.

TIP

Limit the Type of Clip You're Looking For
You can better target your search by choosing a particular clip-art collection from the **Search in** drop-down list, or by choosing a media file type from the **Results should be** list, before clicking Go.

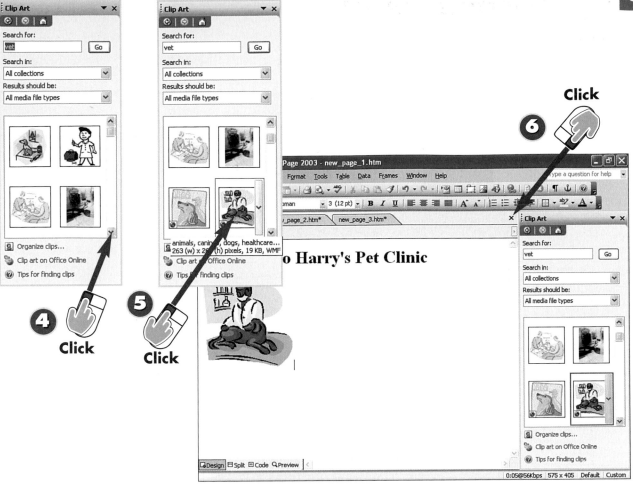

4 Use the scrollbar in the task pane to scroll through the pictures shown.

5 When you see a picture you like, click it once to insert it in your page.

6 The picture is added to your page. Click the **Close** (×) button in the task pane's upper-right corner to close it.

End

HINT

You Can Change a Clip Any Way You Want To
After you insert a clip, you can change that clip's appearance or position in any of the ways described later in this part, including changing the clip's size, repositioning it, or giving it a border.

TIP

There's Still More Clip Art Online
Click the **Clip art on Office Online** link that appears at the bottom of the Clip Art task pane. That link opens your default Web browser and Internet connection, and goes to a Microsoft Web site where you can find additional clips.

Inserting a Picture from a File

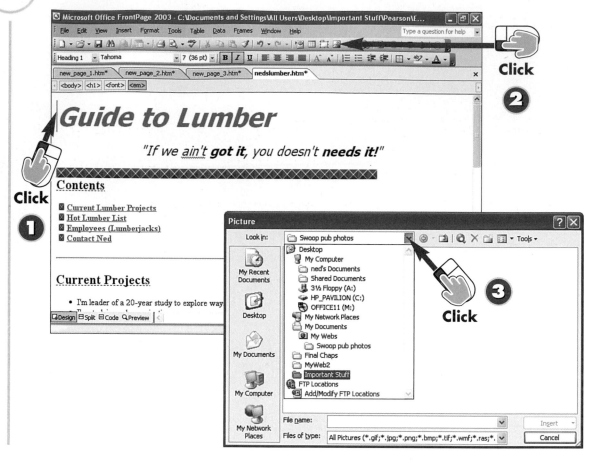

Start

Click

2

Click

1

Click

3

1. Open the Web page in Design view and click at the spot where you want to insert the picture.

2. Click the **Insert Picture from File** button on the Standard toolbar.

3. The Picture dialog box opens. Use the **Look in** list to navigate to the folder where the picture is stored.

INTRODUCTION

Got a picture file of your own that you want to drop in your page? If so, this task is for you. (If not, the next three tasks will help you get one.) Ideally, any picture file you use in a Web page will be in GIF or JPEG file format (that is, using the file extension .gif or .jpg), but you can use pictures stored in just about any file format, including PNG, BMP, TIF, PCX, WMF, and others.

TIP

Just Get the Clip in the Ballpark
Don't worry too much about exactly where you position the picture. After inserting it, you can fine-tune its location, size, shape, and more, as you learn to do later in this part.

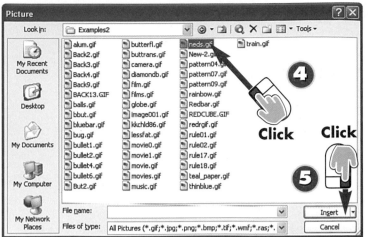

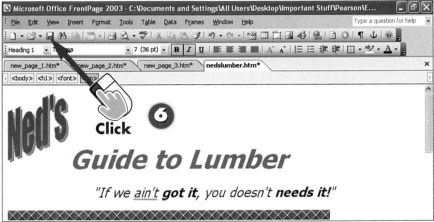

4 Click the picture's name to select it.

5 Click **OK**.

6 The image is inserted in the spot you specified. Click the **Save** button on the Standard toolbar to save the change to the page.

7 When you save the page, a dialog box might appear to report that the picture files will be copied to the same folder as the Web page file. Click **OK**.

End

FrontPage Converts Pictures to GIF

Picture files you've inserted that are not already in GIF or JPEG format are automatically converted to GIF when FrontPage copies them to the Web page's folder.

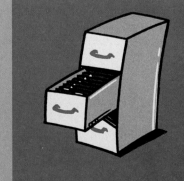

Adding a Picture from a Scanner or Digital Camera

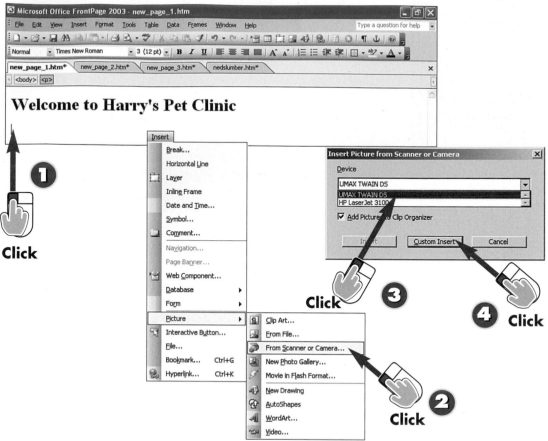

Start

Click

Click

Click

Click

1 Open the Web page in FrontPage's Design view, and click the spot where you want the picture.

2 Open the **Insert** menu, choose **Picture**, and choose **From Scanner or Camera**.

3 Click your scanner or camera in the **Device** list.

4 Click the **Custom Insert** button to open the software that came with the camera or scanner you chose.

Got a scanner or a digital camera? Then you can scan pictures directly into your Web pages in FrontPage 2003, or copy pictures directly from your camera (or its software) into FrontPage.

Set Up Your Camera or Scanner First
This task assumes that you have already connected your scanner or camera to your PC and set up any software it requires.

TWAIN Devices
If your device's software installs in Windows as a TWAIN-compliant device but is not actually TWAIN-compliant, these steps might not work for you. Use the software that came with our device for use on your page.

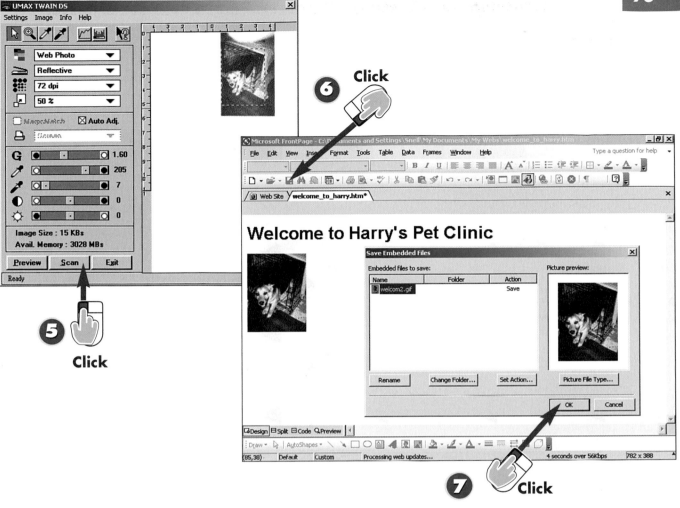

5 In your scanner or camera program, choose among your options for scanning (if you have a scanner) or saving (if you have a camera), and then scan or save.

6 After you scan or save, the picture appears in your page. Click the **Save** button in the Standard toolbar.

7 When you save the page, a dialog box might appear to report that the picture files will be copied to the same folder as the Web page file. Click **OK**.

End

Actual Steps May Vary...
Steps 5 and 6 will vary, depending on whether you have a scanner or camera, and depending on the specific steps to open and scan (or save) pictures in the software that came with your scanner or camera.

Choose the Right Resolution for Web Pics
Most scanners can capture images at higher resolutions and color depths than necessary for the Web. In step 5, use your scanning software to dial down to Web-appropriate scan settings: 72 dpi resolution, 256 colors.

Replacing a Picture

Start

Click

Click

Click

Click

Click

1 Click the picture to select it. *Handles*—little squares—appear around the picture to show it's selected.

2 Click the **Insert Picture from File** button.

3 The Picture dialog box opens. Navigate to the folder that contains the picture you want to add, click the picture file to select it, and click the **Insert** button.

4 The new picture replaces the old one.

End

TIP

Deleting Pictures
To delete a picture without replacing it, just click it to select it, and then press the **Delete** key on your keyboard.

HINT

Deselecting a Picture
To deselect a picture after working with it, just click anywhere in the page except on the picture.

Changing the Size of a Picture

Start

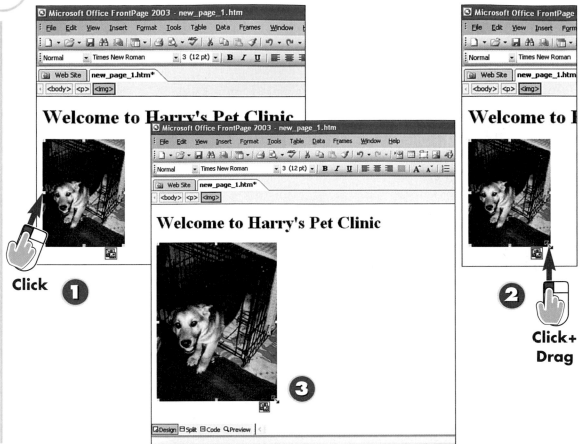

Click ❶

❷ **Click+ Drag**

❸

❶ Click the picture to select it. *Handles* appear around the picture to show it's selected.

❷ Click and hold on a corner handle—*not* a side, top, or bottom handle—and drag toward the picture's center (to shrink it) or away from the center (to enlarge it).

❸ Release the mouse button when the picture is the desired size.

End

Changing the Shape of a Picture

Start

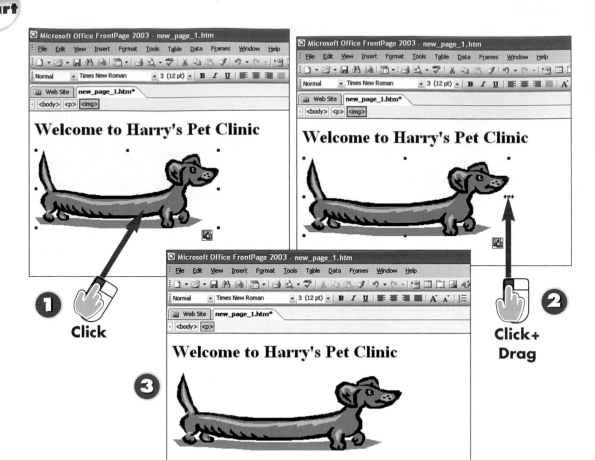

Click

Click+ Drag

1. Click the picture to select it and display its handles.

2. Click and drag a side handle (to change width) or top or bottom handle (to change height) toward the picture's center (to reduce width or height) or away from center (to increase width or height).

3. Release the mouse button when the picture is the desired shape.

End

TIP

Undo Erases All Mistakes

Don't like the way the picture looks after you reshape it? Don't fiddle with trying to drag it back into shape. Just click **Undo**. If that doesn't work, see the task "Undoing Everything You've Done to a Picture" later in this part.

Cropping a Picture

Start

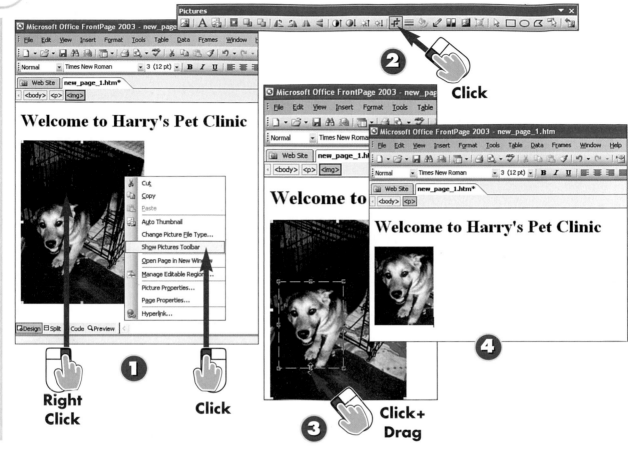

② **Click**

Click

Right Click

Click

③ **Click+ Drag**

④

① Right-click the picture and choose **Show Pictures Toolbar** from the shortcut menu that appears.

② Click the **Crop** button on the Pictures toolbar. A dashed line appears around the image, showing its own set of cropping handles.

③ Click on a cropping handle and drag toward the center of the image. When the dashed lines frame the part of the image you want to keep, click the **Crop** button again.

④ The picture is cropped

End

Whenever you can, you should *crop* a picture—trim unwanted regions off the sides, top, and bottom—in the program in which it was created before inserting it in a page. But when that's not possible, FrontPage lets you trim up a picture right in Design view.

TIP

Cropping from the Corners
To crop both one side and the top or bottom in one move, click and hold on a corner handle in step 3.

Rotating or Flipping a Picture

Start

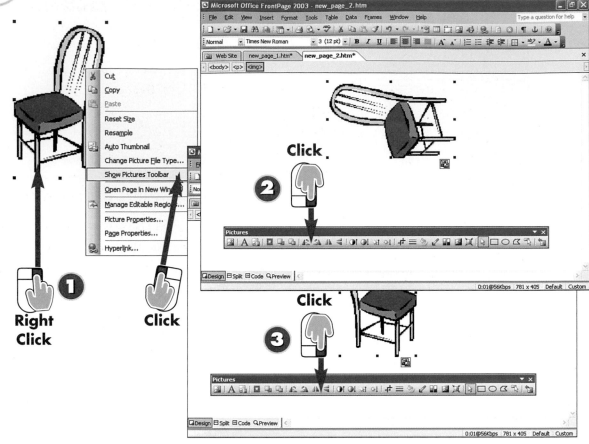

1 Right-click the picture and choose **Show Pictures Toolbar** in the shortcut menu that appears.

2 Click the **Rotate Left** or **Rotate Right** button on the Pictures toolbar to rotate 90 degrees. (Click again to go another 90 degrees.)

3 Click the **Flip Horizontal** or **Flip Vertical** button to reverse the image.

End

INTRODUCTION

So you've got a picture that's just what you want, except it's sideways, upside down, or backward (or it's fine, but you *want* it to be sideways, upside down, or backward). No problem. *Rotating* can turn a sideways or upside down picture the right way, and *flipping* a picture reverses it.

Quick Guide to Flip/Rotate Fixes

TIP

If the picture is upside down (but *not* backward), click a **Rotate** button (either one will do) twice. If the picture is upside down *and* backward, click **Flip Vertical** once. If the picture is backward but *not* upside down, click **Flip Horizontal** once.

Changing the Contrast or Brightness of a Picture

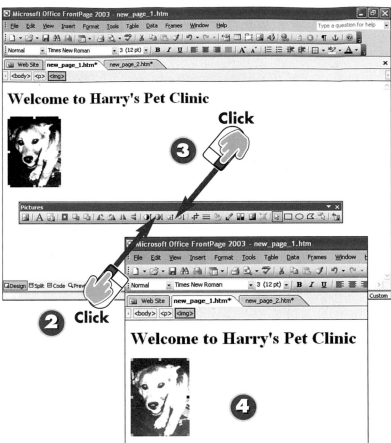

1 Right-click the picture and choose **Show Pictures Toolbar** in the shortcut menu that appears.

2 Click the **More Contrast** or **Less Contrast** button on the Pictures toolbar to adjust the picture's contrast.

3 To adjust the brightness level, click the **More Brightness** or **Less Brightness** button.

4 The image's brightness is adjusted.

End

INTRODUCTION

With some types of picture files, you can adjust *contrast* and brightness with FrontPage. Changing these qualities can dramatically improve the image. Note that this won't work with very simple graphical images, but often works with photos or other images that contain many different shades.

HINT

Clicking Multiple Times Amplifies the Effect
You can click any of these buttons multiple times to amplify the effect applied.

HINT

What If Changing Contrast and Brightness Shows No Effect?
If you click any of these buttons several times in a row and see no apparent change in the picture, the picture is of a type whose brightness and contrast cannot be adjusted.

Changing to Grayscale or "Washing Out" Color

Start

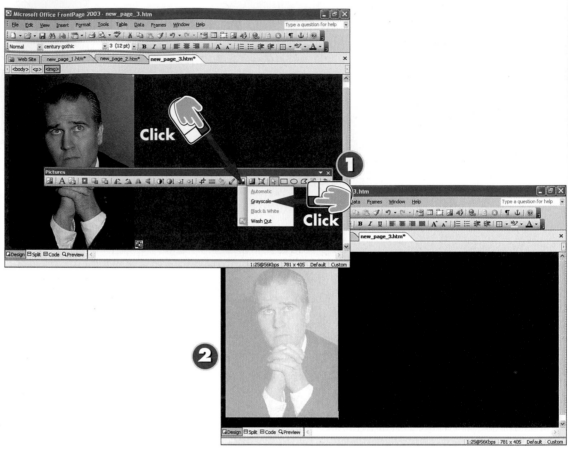

① Click the **Color** button on the Pictures toolbar, and choose **Grayscale** or **Wash Out**.

② The desired effect is applied.

End

On the Web, where so many authors assault you with color overkill, carefully selected grayscale images—such as a black-and-white TV image—add a touch of class. Another cool effect is "washing out"—fading the colors in a picture so that they're softer, more muted. In FrontPage, you can easily apply either of these elegant effects to any picture.

TIP

Graying or Washing Out Could Require Fine-Tuning Brightness/Contrast
After going to gray or washing out, you might want to adjust the picture's contrast and/or brightness (see the preceding task).

Giving a Picture a Transparent Background

Start

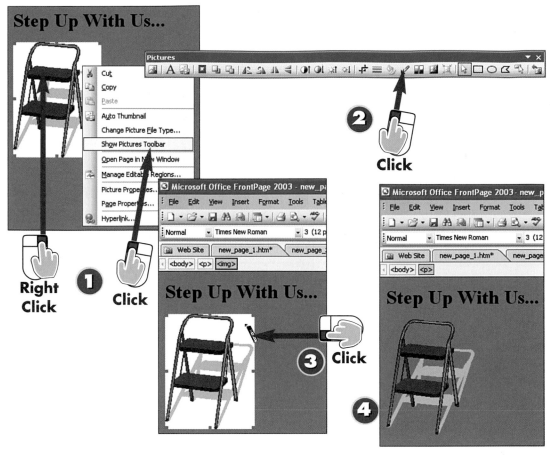

End

1 Right-click the picture and choose **Show Pictures Toolbar**.

2 Click the **Set Transparent Color** button on the Pictures toolbar.

3 Carefully point to the picture's background, and click.

4 The picture's background becomes transparent, making the page background visible.

Undoing Everything You've Done to a Picture

Start

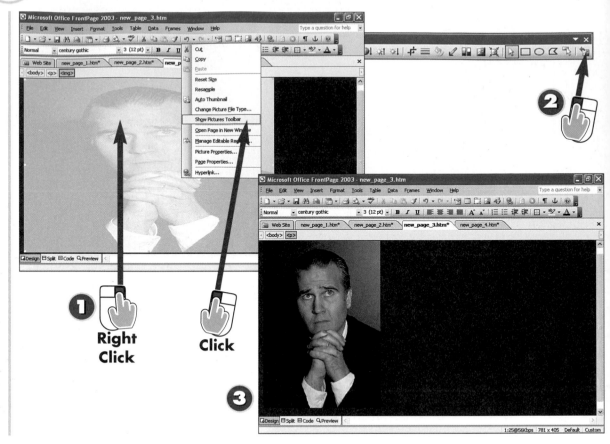

Right Click

Click

1. Right-click the picture and choose **Show Pictures Toolbar**.

2. Click the **Restore** button on the Pictures toolbar.

3. The picture is restored to its original form.

End

INTRODUCTION

Sometimes you'll monkey around with a picture so much that you wind up wishing you could erase all your changes and restore the original, unaltered picture. In such cases, issuing the Undo command often won't work—too many changes under the bridge. But in just two steps, you can remove any and all changes you made to a picture.

TIP

Use Undo to Selectively Reverse Changes to Pictures
If you want to remove some, but not all, of the changes you've made to a picture, use the **Undo** list or selectively change the formatting however you want.

Choosing a Picture's Alignment

Start

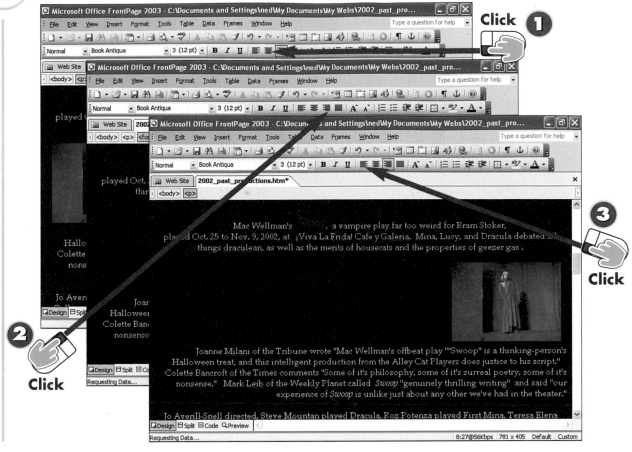

Click **1**

Click **2**

Click **3**

Click

1 After you click the picture to select it, click the **Center** button on the Formatting toolbar.

2 The picture is centered on the page. To right-align it, click the **Right Align** button on the Formatting toolbar.

3 The picture is right-aligned on the page. To left-align it, click the **Left Align** button on the Formatting toolbar.

End

INTRODUCTION

By default, a picture you insert goes on the left side of the page. But you can center it or align it to the right side of the page, exactly as you do text.

Pictures Are Paragraphs

TIP

For all intents and purposes, a picture is a paragraph. That means that you can not only use the Alignment buttons to align it as you would a text paragraph, but also that you can indent pictures with the **Increase Indent** button.

Changing the Position of a Picture

Start

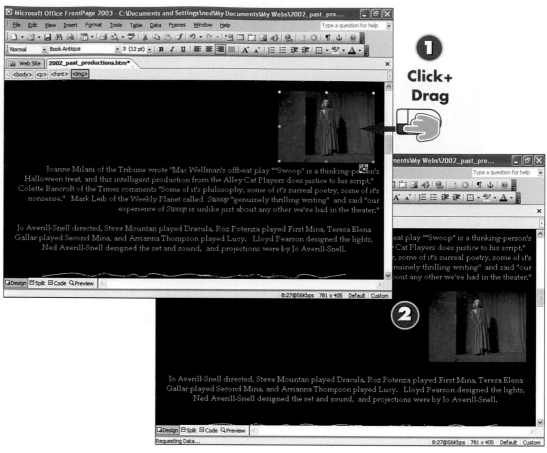

①
Click+
Drag

②

① Click the picture and drag it to where you want it. (A little square icon follows the pointer to tell you you're dragging something.)

② When the square icon is in the spot where you want the picture to be placed, release the mouse button. The picture is moved.

End

Generally, you position a picture only in the ways you position a paragraph; it can go at the top of the page, at the bottom, or between any two paragraphs, and it can be aligned to the left, right, or center. There are exceptions, which you'll explore in the next three tasks; here are the simple steps for moving a picture from one general location to another.

TIP

If you prefer, you can move a picture using FrontPage's Cut and Paste commands, just like you do text. Select the picture, click the **Cut** button, click in the new spot, and click the **Paste** button.

Wrapping Text to a Picture

Start

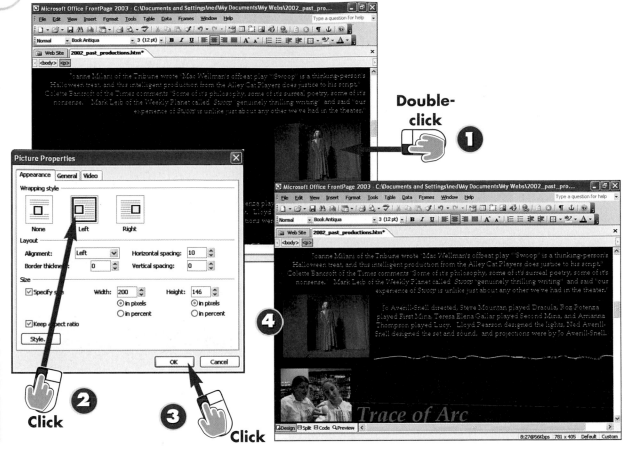

Double-click **1**

Click **2**

Click **3**

4

1 Double-click the picture to open the **Picture Properties** dialog box.

2 On the Appearance tab, click **None**, **Left**, or **Right** in the **Wrapping style** area to choose the kind of wrapping style you want.

3 Click **OK**.

4 The text is wrapped in the style you selected.

End

INTRODUCTION

When text comes right after a picture, you can choose the relationship between the text and picture. For example, should the text start below the image, to the right of it, or to the left of it?

TIP

Cutting and Pasting
You can't use a wrapping style with a picture that's *absolutely positioned* (see the next task). If you do, the absolute positioning is removed automatically, and the picture reverts to standard positioning.

Choosing the "Absolute" Position of a Picture

Start

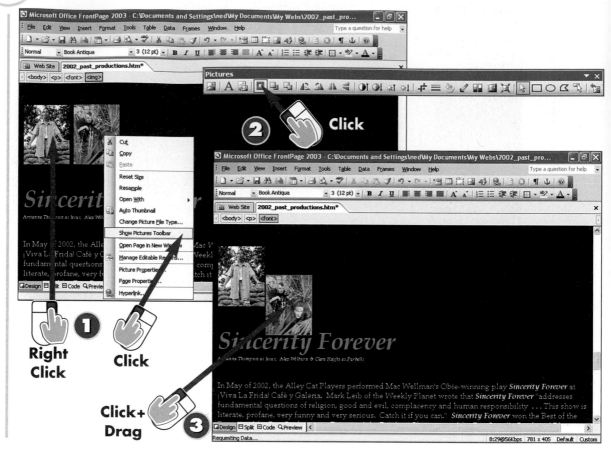

Right Click

Click

Click

Click+ Drag

① Right-click the picture and choose **Show Pictures Toolbar**.

② Click the **Position Absolutely** button on the Pictures toolbar.

③ Drag the picture to any spot you want.

End

As you've seen, pictures plug into your Web page layout in a general way, like big paragraphs, so that you don't have the sort of precise control of where they appear in the layout that you might have in a word processing or desktop publishing program. Using this task, you can position a picture at a precise spot on the page in relation to the outlines of the page itself and all the other elements it contains. You can position pictures so precisely that you can overlap them, or overlap text or tables. This "absolute positioning" gives you far greater control of your page layout. Note, however, that this positioning shows up *only* when the page is viewed through a DHTML-compatible browser, such as Internet Explorer 4 (or later) or Navigator 4 (or later).

HINT

Using Tables
You can get better control of where pictures and other objects appear in the layout—without resorting to absolute positioning—by laying out the page as a big table. See Part 8 for more information.

Layering Pictures

Start

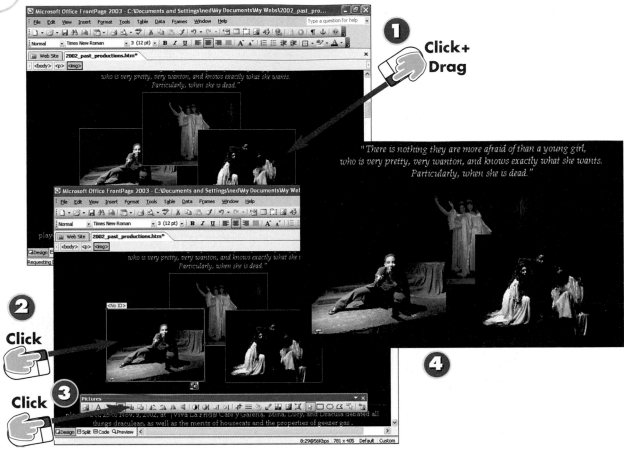

1 Click+ Drag

2 Click

3 Click

4

---

1 With the Picture toolbar displayed, drag your absolutely positioned object or objects on top of one another, in any order.

2 Click any visible portion of the object whose position in the pile you want to change.

3 On the Pictures toolbar, click the **Bring Forward** button to move the object one level closer to the top of the pile, or the **Send Backward** button to move the object one level deeper.

4 The picture is layered accordingly.

End

Putting Multiple Links in a Picture

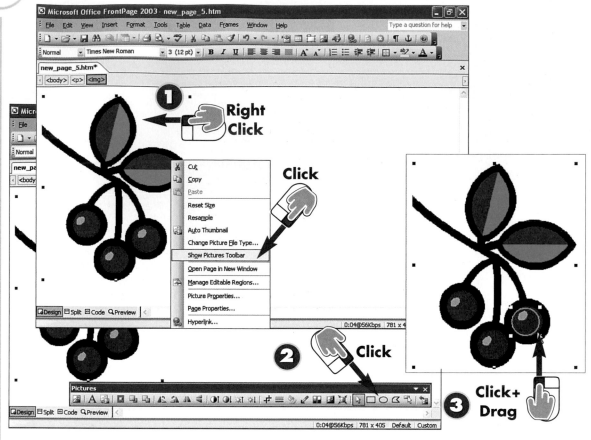

1 Right-click the picture you want to make into an image map and choose **Show Pictures Toolbar**.

2 Click the **Rectangular**, **Circular**, or **Polygonal Hotspot** button.

3 Point to a spot on the picture in or near where the link should go. Click and drag outward to create the hotspot, and release (you'll fine-tune its size and position later).

INTRODUCTION

A picture containing multiple links is called an *image map*. The word to remember is *hotspots*—invisible boxes on the picture, each of which has a link attached to it. Use a picture that has easily identifiable regions in it so that visitors don't have to guess where the links are.

TIP

Using the Polygonal Hotspot Tool
When using the Polygonal hotspot tool, click and drag to draw the first line. Click again and drag to draw the next, and so on. When drawing the last line, make sure that you draw all the way to the start of your first line (closing the shape) and click.

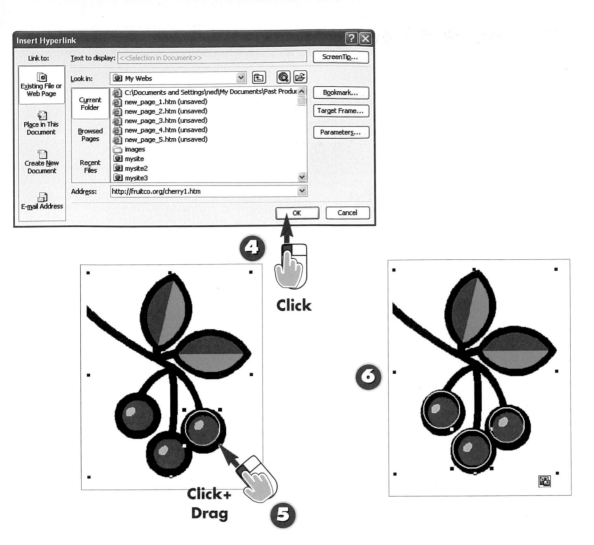

Click

Click+ Drag 5

4 In the **Insert Hyperlink** dialog box, specify the Web page, email address, file, or other element that you want to link to (refer to Part 5 for help) and then click **OK**.

5 Adjust the hotspot so that its size and position more or less fit the region (see the tip on this page for help resizing and repositioning hotspots).

6 Repeat steps 2–5 for each link in the picture, creating a separate hotspot for each.

End

Resizing and Repositioning Hotspots
To resize a hotspot, drag the hotspot's handles as you would when resizing a picture. To fine-tune a polygonal hotspot, drag the handles at its corners. To move a hotspot, click anywhere within the hotspot, drag it to the new location, and release the mouse button.

Changing a Hotspot's Link
To change a hotspot's link, double-click the hotspot and use the Edit Hyperlink dialog box as you learned in Part 5. To delete a hotspot, click it to select it, and then press the **Delete** key on your keyboard.

Creating a Photo Gallery

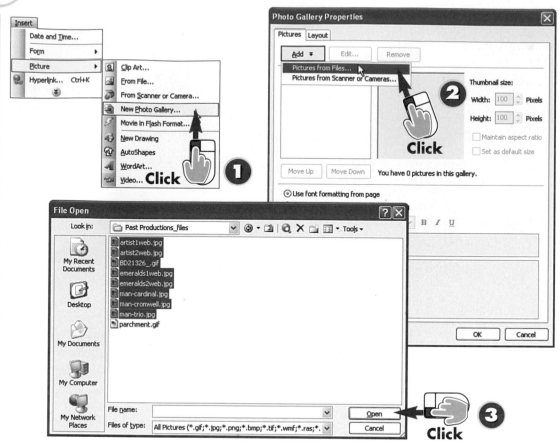

1 Click the spot in a Web page where you want to add a photo gallery, and choose **Insert**, **Picture**, **New Photo Gallery**.

2 The Photo Gallery Properties dialog box opens. Click the **Add** button, and choose **Pictures from Files**.

3 The File Open dialog box opens. Navigate to the folder where the picture files are stored, select the picture files you want to use, and click the **Open** button.

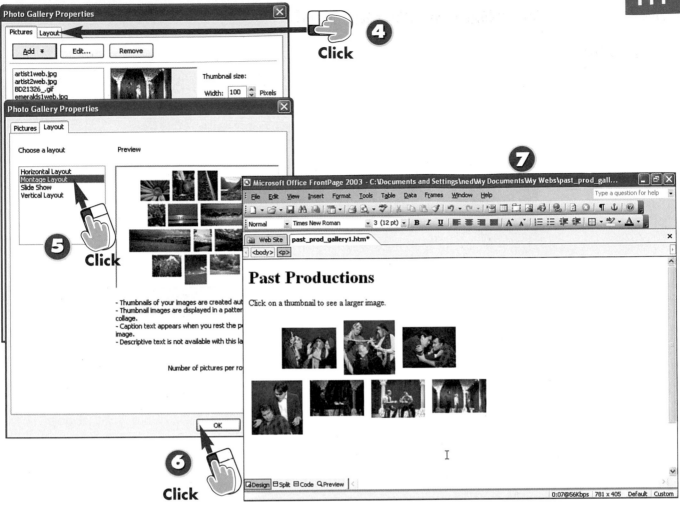

④ In the Photo Gallery Properties dialog box, click the **Layout** tab.

⑤ Choose a layout for your gallery.

⑥ Click **OK**.

⑦ The gallery is created. Save your page and continue to edit it any way you want.

End

FrontPage Saves the Pic Files with the Page
FrontPage automatically saves the pictures with the Web page and copies the thumbnails and the full versions of the photos to the Web when you publish. (FrontPage may display a box telling you this when you save.)

Double-Click the Gallery to Change It, Anytime
To change your gallery or its appearance anytime, double-click on it to open the Photo Gallery Properties dialog box and change whatever you want—even the list of pictures.

Preview Your Page to Test Your Gallery
To test your gallery—so that you can click the thumbnails and see the full pictures appear—preview the page.

Using Borders, Backgrounds, Sounds, and More

Most Web pages contain nothing more than text, pictures, and links, so that's where this book has been concentrated thus far. Beyond those types of Web content, however, is a motley assortment of other things you may or may not want to add to your page, often just for kicks. You're a fan of miscellany? Lucky you—you're about to learn how to add backgrounds, picture borders, sounds, video, and other odds and ends to your pages.

FrontPage's *themes* (see Part 2) control some items you'll learn how to modify in this part, such as the background and text colors. If you are using a theme for your page or site and you want to change the background or colors, it's usually best to change these items by changing the theme, rather than changing these items individually in pages, as described here.

Borders, Backgrounds, Sounds, and More

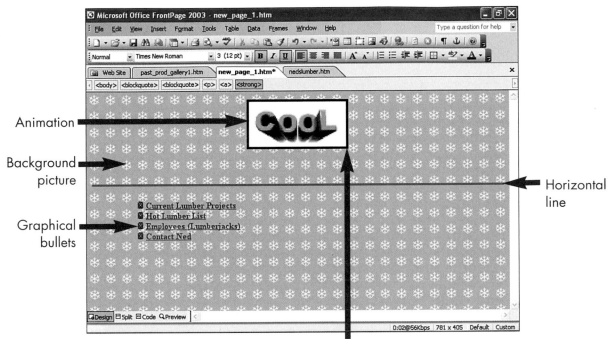

Choosing Background and Text Colors

Start

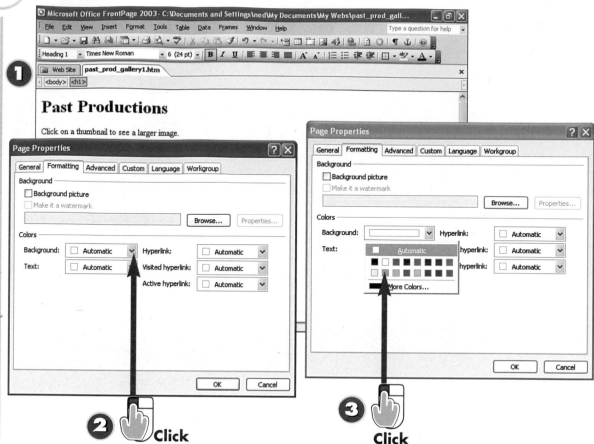

2 Click

3 Click

1 With the page to which you want to apply a background color displayed onscreen, open the **Format** menu and choose **Background**.

2 The Page Properties dialog box opens, with the Formatting tab displayed. Click the **down arrow** next to the **Background** field.

3 Click the square containing the color you want to use (or click **More Colors** to choose from a palette that offers a wider selection).

You can choose any color for a page's background, or you can use a picture for a background (see the next task). While choosing a background color, it's smart to consider choosing text colors at the same time to ensure that the text colors are a good contrast to the background. (Text in a color that's too close to the background color is difficult to see.)

TIP

Do It Differently If You're Using a Theme

If you've assigned a theme to this page, you should change background and text colors from the Themes dialog box (see Part 2) instead of doing this task.

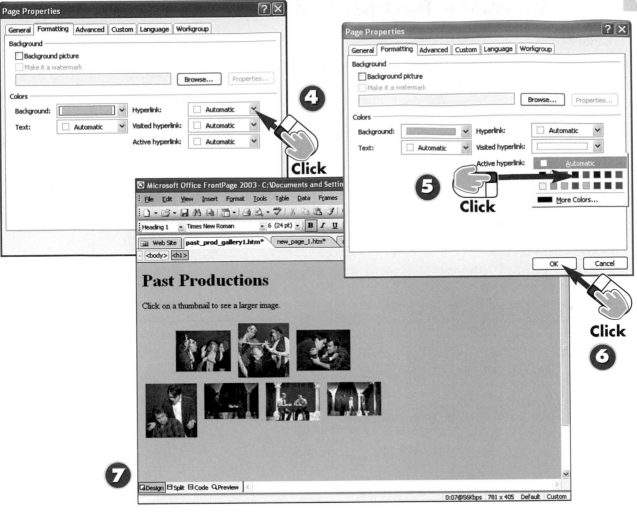

4 Determine whether the colored squares in the **Text** field and in the three **Hyperlink** fields contrast well with the background color (and with each other).

5 Use the list boxes to change text colors as necessary.

6 Click **OK**.

7 The background color (and any other colors you selected) is applied.

Users May Block Your Custom Color Choices
Users can configure their browsers to reject the "custom" text and background colors you choose here and show the same colors for all pages instead. Users who do this will not see the text colors you choose, but will see the text itself just fine.

Use Font Color to Override Default Colors
After choosing the default color for each kind of text, you can still assign any color you want to selected text by clicking the **Font Color** button on the Formatting toolbar.

Using a Picture Background

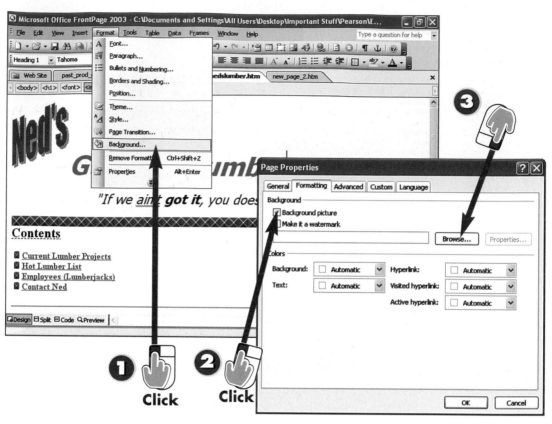

Start

Click **Click**

1 With the page to which you want to apply a background picture displayed onscreen, open the **Format** menu and choose **Background**.

2 The Page Properties dialog box opens with the Formatting tab displayed. Click to put a check in the **Background Picture** checkbox.

3 To locate the picture file you want to use as the background, click the **Browse** button.

Instead of using a solid-color background, as you learned to do in the preceding task, you can use a picture as a background. If the picture is too small to fill the whole window in which the page appears, it is automatically *tiled*—repeated over and over—to fill the window. Tiling enables you to build a great-looking pattern out of the repeated image.

INTRODUCTION

HINT

Picture Backgrounds Trump Color Backgrounds
An image background automatically supersedes a background color. If you create an image background, any selection you might have made for background color is irrelevant.

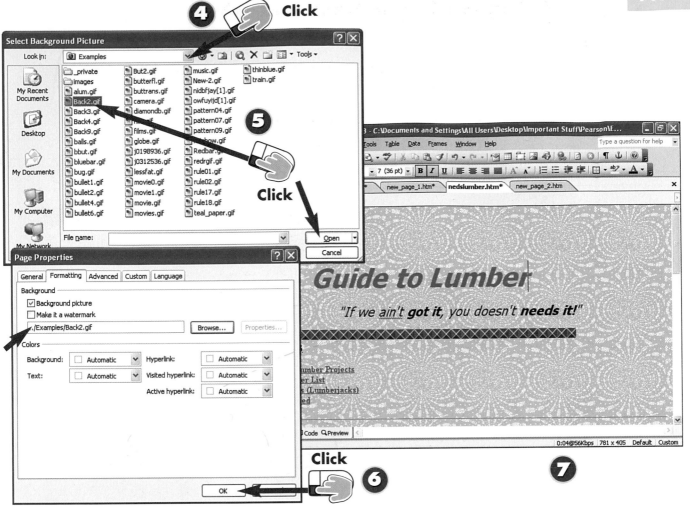

4. The Select Background Picture dialog box opens. Navigate to the folder containing the image you want to use as a background.

5. Click the desired image to select it. Click the **Open** button.

6. The path to the selected image appears in the field. Click **OK**.

7. The background image is applied.

End

Watch Out for Big Files
An image background, like any picture file, slows the downloading of your page, so avoid using very large background files. A large background image slows down the page's download much more than a small picture tiled many times.

Multiple Small Images "Tile" to Make One Background
You can get background image files that are specially designed so that, when tiled, they form a seamless texture, such as marble or wood. The Clip Art Gallery has several such images in its Web Backgrounds category.

Putting a Border Around a Picture

Start

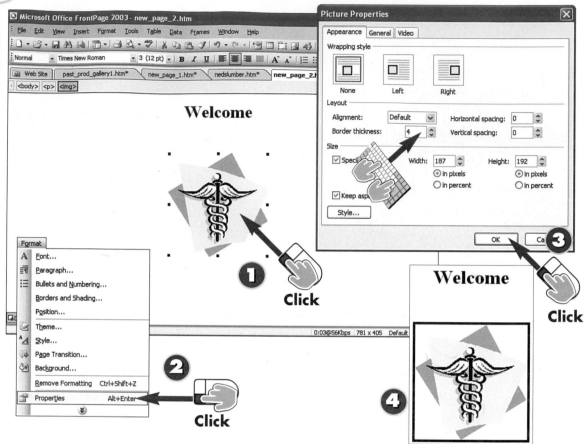

Welcome

1 Click

2 Click

3 Click

Welcome

1 Click the picture to which you want to add a border to select it.

2 Open the **Format** menu and choose **Properties**. The Picture Properties dialog box opens.

3 In the **Border thickness** field, type a number or click the up or down arrow to set the border thickness (a higher number makes a thicker border), and click **OK**.

4 The border is applied.

End

Adding a Bevel

Start

✂	Cut
📋	Copy
📋	Paste
📑	Auto Thumbnail
	Change Picture File Type...
	Show Pictures Toolbar
	Open Page in New Window
	Manage Editable Regions...
	Picture Properties...
	Page Properties...
🔗	Hyperlink...

2 Click

1 Click

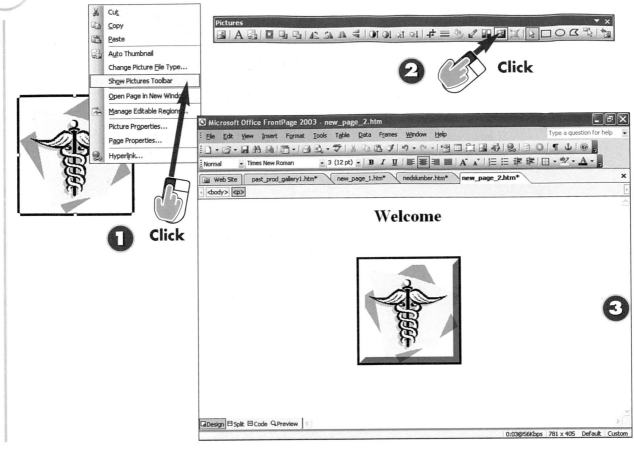

3

End

---

1 Right-click the selected picture and choose **Show Pictures Toolbar** in the shortcut menu that appears.

2 Click the **Bevel** button on the Pictures toolbar.

3 The bevel is applied.

You can add a 3D effect to a picture's border by adding a *bevel*, a gray shadow along the bottom and right side. A bevel creates the illusion that the picture is floating above the page. It's a nice touch, if you don't overuse it.

Bevels Don't Require Borders

You can add a bevel to a picture that has its own built-in border, or to any square or rectangular picture. The bevel really has nothing to do with the border, but a bevel without some sort of apparent border on the other two sides looks a little odd.

Organizing Pages with Horizontal Lines

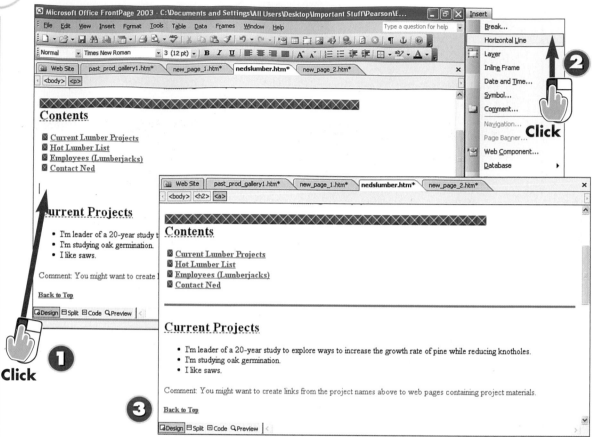

1 Click in your page at the spot where you want to insert the line.

2 Open the **Insert** menu and choose **Horizontal Line**.

3 The line is inserted in the spot you selected.

Horizontal lines help divide a page visually. Used between a heading and the paragraph that follows it, a line can add a little extra style to page. Lines also help divide sections of a longer page. Best of all, they're incredibly easy to insert, and they add graphical flair without slowing the download of the page the way pictures can.

Fancier Lines Aren't Horizontal Lines—They're Pictures

Online, you'll see all sorts of fancy multicolor lines dividing up pages. These aren't real horizontal lines; they're pictures used like lines, and you insert them like any other picture. You can find a great selection of these in Clip Gallery's Web Dividers category. Note that, unlike real horizontal lines, picture lines can't automatically scale themselves to a percentage of the width of the page. So when using picture lines, make sure that the line is of a width that still looks good no matter what resolution the visitor views the page in.

Changing the Look of a Line

Start

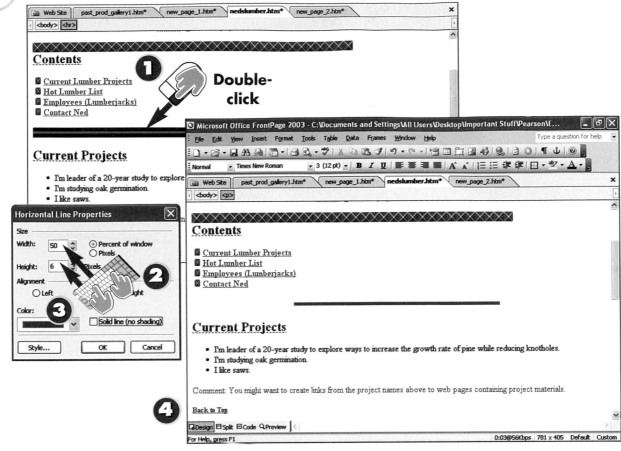

1 **Double-click**

2

3

4

1 Double-click a line you've inserted to open the Horizontal Line Properties dialog box.

2 To make the line shorter, type a value less than 100 in the **Width** field. Type a number in the **Height** field to change the thickness; a higher number makes a thicker line.

3 Choose an **Alignment** and **Color** and then click **OK**.

4 The changes you specified are applied to the line.

End

Adding a basic horizontal line is a snap. But with just a little extra effort, you can change that line's appearance, making it thicker or thinner, making it shorter, and choosing its alignment and color.

TIP

You Can Turn the 3D Effect On or Off
By default, the line has a shadow under it to give it a 3D effect. To remove the shadow, click the **Solid line** check box to deselect it.

Playing a Background Sound

Start

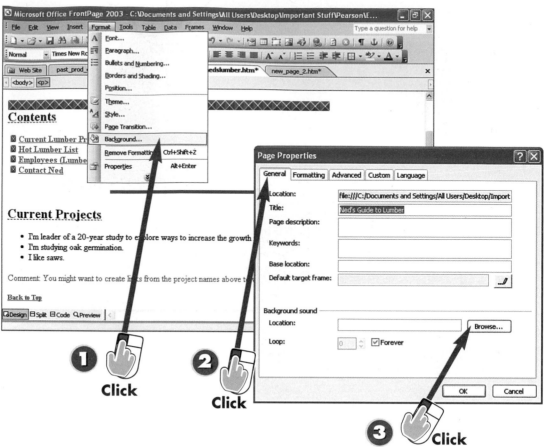

1 With the page to which you want to apply a sound effect displayed onscreen, open the **Format** menu and choose **Background**.

2 The Page Properties dialog box opens. Click the **General** tab.

3 Click the **Browse** button.

For a nice touch, you can make a sound effect or music clip play the moment a visitor arrives at a page. Only users of Internet Explorer 3 or later will hear the clip, so don't make the clip an essential part of understanding your page. Consider it a nice "throw-in" for the IE crowd.

You Can Use Any Sound File Type

Sound clips in WAV format (.wav) work best, but you can use clips stored in other formats. To use a non-WAV file, between steps 3 and 4, open the **Files of type** list in the Select File dialog box and choose the file type you will use.

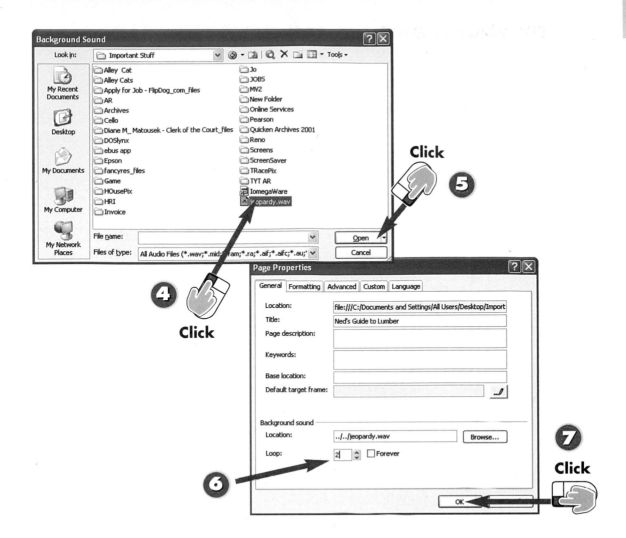

4 Navigate to the sound clip file you want to use, and click it to select it.

5 Click the **Open** button.

6 Mark the **Forever** check box to make the clip play for as long as the visitor views the page. Or type the number of times to play the sound in the **Loop** field.

7 Click **OK**.

End

Preview to Hear Your Sounds
Sounds don't play in Design view; to hear the background sound, preview the page.

Record Your Own Sound Clips
By connecting a microphone or other audio source to your PC's sound card, you can record your own sound clips using Windows's built-in recorder. To access the recorder, click the **Start** button, choose **Programs**, select **Accessories**, click **Entertainment**, and choose **Sound Recorder**.

Adding Animation from the Clip Gallery

Start

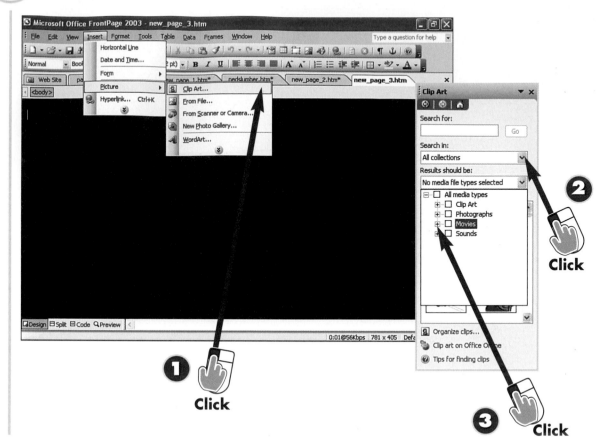

1 Click in your page where you want to insert the animation. Open the **Insert** menu, choose **Picture**, and then choose **Clip Art**.

2 The Clip Art task pane opens. Click the **down arrow** next to the **Results should be** field and click each check box in the list to uncheck it.

3 Click the **+** sign next to the **Movies** entry in the **Results Should Be** list to open the list of movie file types.

A special kind of GIF image file, called an *animated GIF*, plays a brief, simple animation when you view it in a Web page. You'll find animated GIFs in clip-art libraries online and on disk, and you can create them with programs such as Macromedia Flash. You'll find a bunch in FrontPage's clip-art library.

HINT

Preview to See Your Animations Move
Note that your animation won't play in Design view; to see the animation play in your page, preview the page.

Click 4

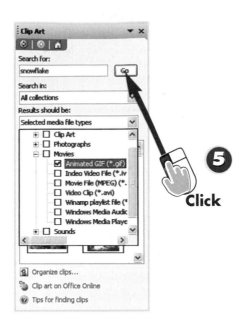

Click 5

4 Check the check box next to **Animated GIF** to mark it.

5 Now use the **Search for** field and **Go** button to search for and select your clip to insert it, as described in the very first task of Part 6.

End

Previewing an Animation Before Using It

To see the animation play before you insert it, point to it in the task pane list to display an arrow along its right side, click the arrow, and then choose **Preview/Properties** from the menu that appears.

Just Like Any Other GIF

You change the size, shape, position, and other aspects of an animated GIF exactly as you would a regular GIF (refer to Part 6).

Using Graphical Bullets

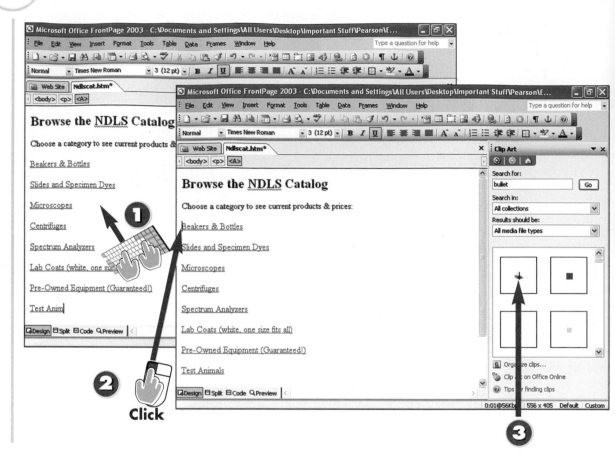

Click

1. Type the list items as ordinary paragraphs, pressing **Enter** after each. (*Do not* click the Bullets button!)

2. Click to the left of the first item.

3. Insert the picture file you'll use as a bullet, any way you want (from a file, from the Clip Gallery, by scanning, and so on; see Part 6 for help).

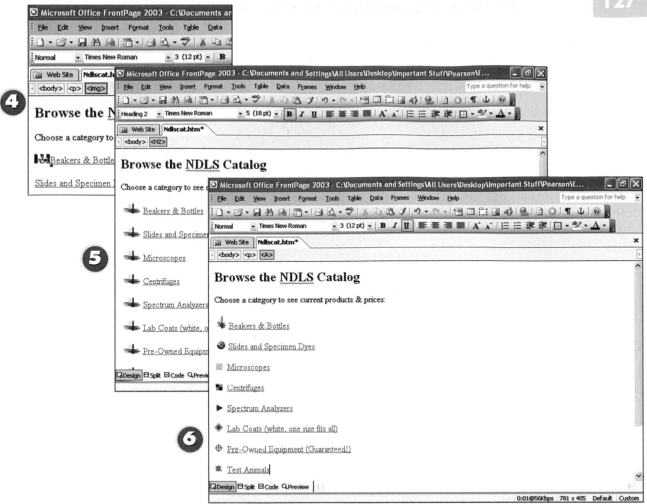

4 Format the bullet picture as desired (size, shape, and so on).

5 To use the same bullet for other list items, copy the bullet (select it and click the **Copy** button) and paste it in front of each item in the list (click the **Paste** button).

6 To use a different bullet picture on each item, repeat steps 2–4 for each item.

Indenting Your Bulleted List
To indent the finished list (after adding the bullets), click to the left of the bullet on the first item, drag downward to select the whole list—*including* all bullets—and then click the **Increase Indent** button.

Adding Space Between Bullets and List Text
To increase the space between the bullet and the text, right-click the picture, choose **Image Properties**, **Appearance** tab. Increase the number shown in **Horizontal Spacing**, and then click **OK**.

Bullets Can Be Animated
If you use small animated GIFs for bullets, you'll have animated bullets.

Inserting a Video Clip

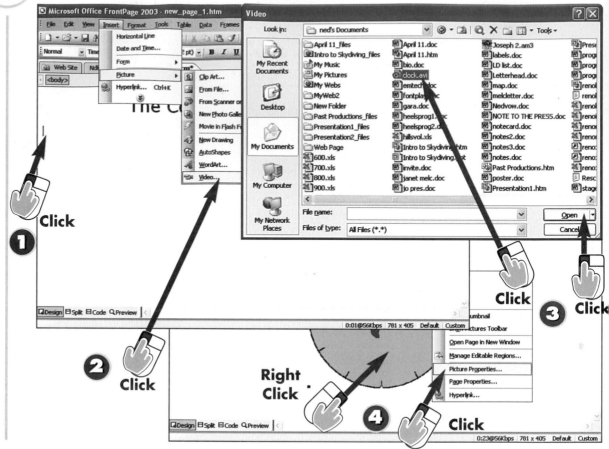

Click ❶

Click ❷

Click ❸

Click

Right Click ❹

Click

❶ Click in your page at the general spot where you want the video clip to appear.

❷ Open the **Insert** menu, choose **Picture**, and choose **Video**.

❸ Navigate to and select the AVI file you want to insert and then click the **Open** button.

❹ A picture representing the video is inserted. Right-click the picture, and choose **Picture Properties** from the shortcut menu.

With a video capture card installed in your PC and a video source (such as a camcorder or VCR), you can create video files in Windows Video (AVI) format. FrontPage makes inserting those clips in your pages easy and presents them attractively as frozen still pictures in the page that play automatically or at the visitor's request.

HINT

Inline Video's Not for Everybody

FrontPage's method of showing the clip "inline" like a picture is viewable only through Internet Explorer 3 or later, and could degrade the performance of the page.

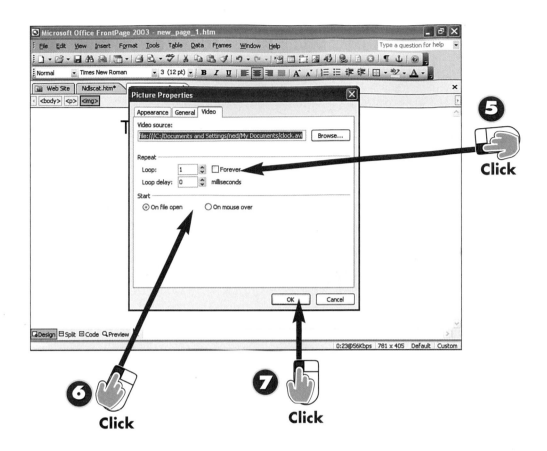

5 To play the video continuously, check the **Forever** check box. To play it a set number of times, type the number of times to play in **Loop**.

6 To play the video as soon as the page appears, click **On file open**. To play the video when the visitor's mouse pointer passes over the picture, click **On mouse over**.

7 Click **OK**.

End

Adding a Pause Between Loops
When the clip will be played repeatedly (*looped*), you can add a brief pause between each loop by entering a number in the **Loop delay** field. The delay is measured in milliseconds (1/1000ths of a second), so a loop delay of 500 adds a half-second pause.

To Watch Your Video Play, Preview
Video doesn't play in Design view; to see the video play in your page, preview the page.

Creating Tables

Web pages offer many tools for organizing content in attractive ways: headings, lists, indentation, alignment, horizontal lines, and wrapping around pictures. But when you have a lot of content—eight or more items—that fall logically into groups, a nice table is the way to go. You can even include gridlines and column headers if you need your table to look like a spreadsheet for data or other information.

Even when your content isn't "tabular" in nature, you'll find that tables come in handy in another way: You can use a big table to design and control the layout of a whole page (as some of FrontPage's templates do).

In this part, you discover how easy it is to make tables in FrontPage 2003, and to make them look great.

Tools for Tables

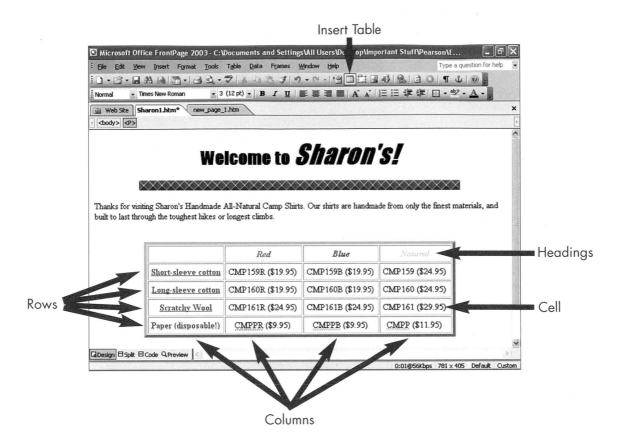

Insert Table

Headings

Cell

Rows

Columns

Inserting a New Table in a Snap

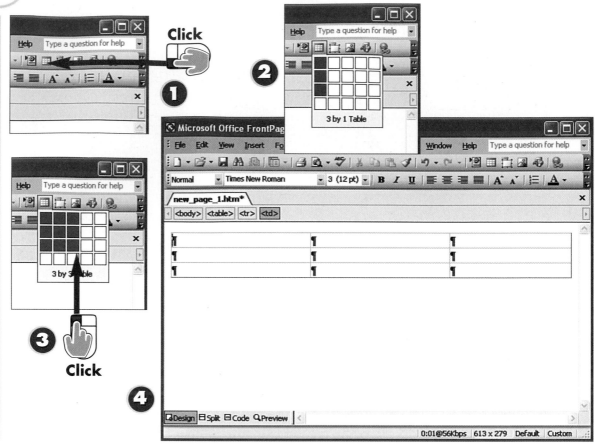

Click

Click

End

1 Click the **Insert Table** button on the Standard toolbar.

2 Move the mouse downward (don't click or hold!) to highlight the number of rows you want.

3 Move the mouse to the right to highlight the number of columns you want, and click.

4 A table with the number of rows and columns you specified is added to your page.

All you need to get started with tables is a page in progress, a rough idea of what you want to put in the table (sometimes it helps to scribble the table out on paper first), and a rough idea of where you want to put it. Here's the quickest way to start a table (as long as it's no bigger than four columns by five rows).

The Dashes Are for Show
Dashed lines seen around table cells in Design view just show where your table is—they won't show up on the Web page. But if you really *want* visible table borders, see the task "Dressing Up Tables with Gridlines" later in this part.

Don't Worry About Size
Don't worry about the size (or number) of the rows and columns in the table initially. The rows and columns will expand to fit your content as you enter it, and you can also manually choose their size. You can add or delete rows and columns, too.

Inserting a More Complex New Table

Start

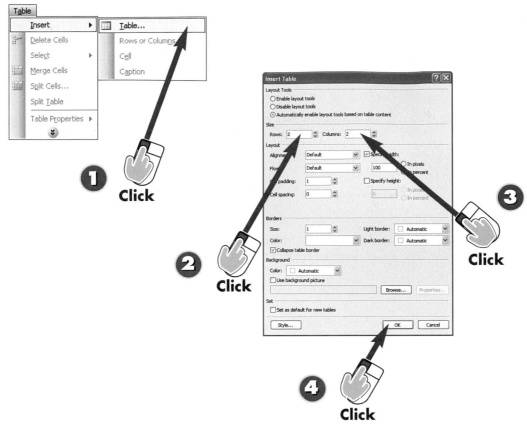

1 Click

2 Click

3 Click

4 Click

1 Open the **Table** menu, choose **Insert**, and select **Table**.

2 In the **Rows** field, type the number of rows the table should contain.

3 In the **Columns** field, type the number of columns the table should contain.

4 Click **OK** or press **Enter**.

End

When the table will be bigger than 4 columns by 5 rows, or when you want to select certain formatting options while creating the table, FrontPage offers an alternative table-creation method.

TIP

Can't See the Whole Table Dialog Box
The Insert Table dialog box is very large; depending on the screen resolution you use on your computer, you might not be able to see the bottom of it, even if you drag it as high as you can. For now, don't worry—everything you need is near the top of the dialog box, except the OK button. If you can't see the OK button, remember that pressing the **Enter** key does the same thing as clicking OK.

Importing a Table from Another Program

Start

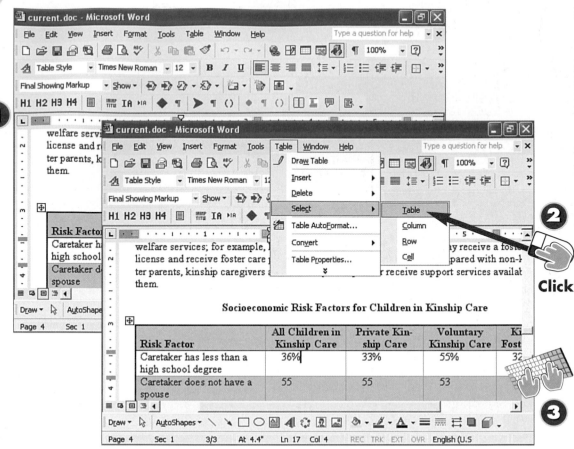

1

2 Click

3

1 In the program you used to create the table you want to import, open the file containing the table (or create the table).

2 If you are using Word, click the table, or open the **Table** menu, and choose **Select**, **Table**; in Excel, highlight the portion of the current worksheet you want to import.

3 Press and hold down the **Ctrl** key, press the **Insert** key, and then release both keyboard buttons.

INTRODUCTION

If you have another Windows program in which you can create tables, such as Microsoft Word or Excel, you can create tables there and then import those tables right into your FrontPage Web pages. This not only enables you to create tables by using programs you already know, but also to easily reuse tables you might already have in word-processing or spreadsheet documents.

There Are Other Ways to Copy

In most programs, instead of step 3, you can click a **Copy** button on the toolbar, or choose **Edit**, **Copy**. But in case those options aren't available, **Ctrl+Insert** always works in Windows programs.

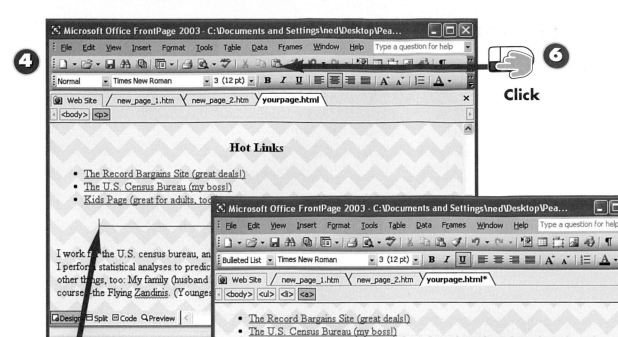

Click

Click

4. Switch to (or open) the FrontPage file, and click the spot on the Web page where you want the table to go.

5. Click the **Paste** button on the Standard toolbar.

6. The table is pasted into your Web page.

End

Change Imported Tables Any Way You Want

TIP

After importing the table, you may edit and enhance the table in any of the ways described in this part, just as if you had created it in FrontPage.

Deleting a Table

Start

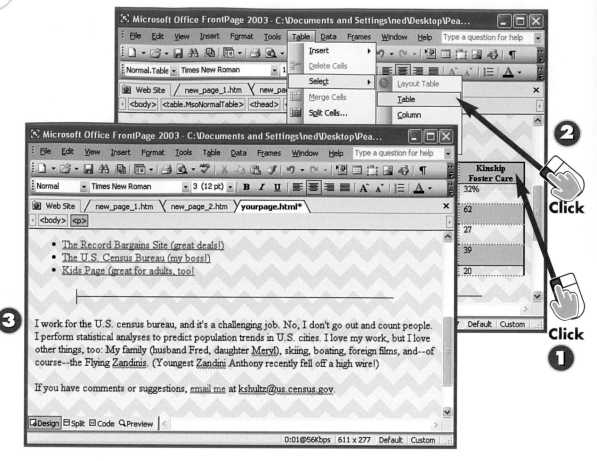

2 Click

Click
1

3

1 Click anywhere in the table you want to delete.

2 Open the **Table** menu, choose **Select**, and then **Table**. Press the **Delete** key on your keyboard.

3 The table is deleted.

End

The Web author who createth hath the power to taketh away. (Or something like that.) Here's how to delete a table.

You Can Drag Tables Where You Want 'Em
To move a table, first perform steps 1 and 2. Then, click and hold on the selected table, drag it where you want it, and release it.

Putting Text in Table Cells

Start

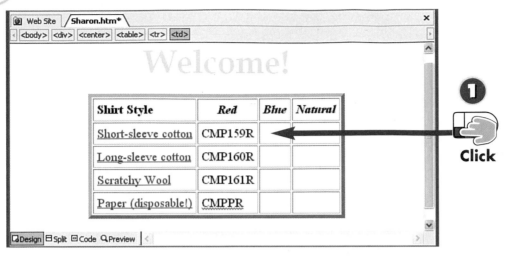

1 Click

1 Click in the cell in which you want to add text.

2 Type whatever you want.

3 Press the **Tab** key to jump to the next cell (or click in the cell you want to fill next), and type the text you want.

End

A table without content is like a room without furniture. Here's how to start filling in your new table by putting text in *cells*—the boxes formed by each intersection of a row and column.

Alignment Aligns Text in the Cell, Not on the Page
If you apply alignment (see Part 4) to text in a cell, the text is aligned relative to the cell it's in, not the page. For example, if you apply center alignment to text in a cell, the text is centered within the cell.

Formatting Table Text
You can apply character formatting including fonts, bold, italic, underlining, or color to text in a table. Making the text in all cells in the top row bold, italic, or a unique color is a nice way to create column headings that stand out.

Putting Pictures in a Table

Start

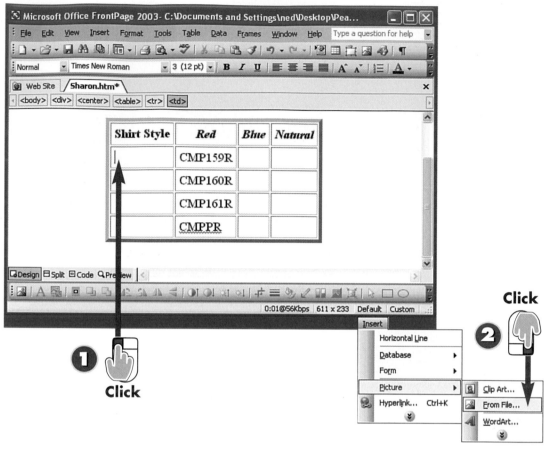

1 Click in the cell in which you want to put a picture.

2 Using any of the techniques mentioned in Part 6, insert the picture.

Most tables are mostly text, but you can give your table panache by using a picture or two in its cells.

TIP

Tables Can Hold Animations
Yes, you *can* put an animated GIF picture in a table cell.

TIP

Links Work in Table Cells
You can put links in a table, too. Just add to the table the text or picture you want to use as the link source, highlight that text or picture in its table cell, and create the link as usual (see Part 5 for more information).

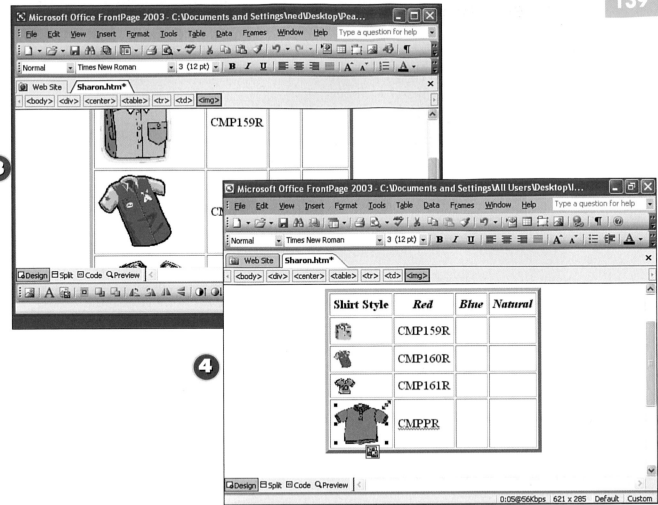

3 Continue adding pictures to cells until you've added all the pictures for this table.

4 On each picture, drag a corner handle (see Part 6) to scale the picture to the size you want.

End

Row and Column Sizes Will Change to Fit Your Pics
When you have sized all the pictures in your table, the row and column sizes automatically change their size to match.

Pictures in Tables Are Fully Formattable
You can use any of the picture-formatting techniques from Part 6 on a picture in a table cell. To open the Image Properties dialog box to format a picture in a cell, point to the picture, right-click, and choose **Picture Properties** from the shortcut menu that appears.

Automatically Filling Multiple Table Cells

Start

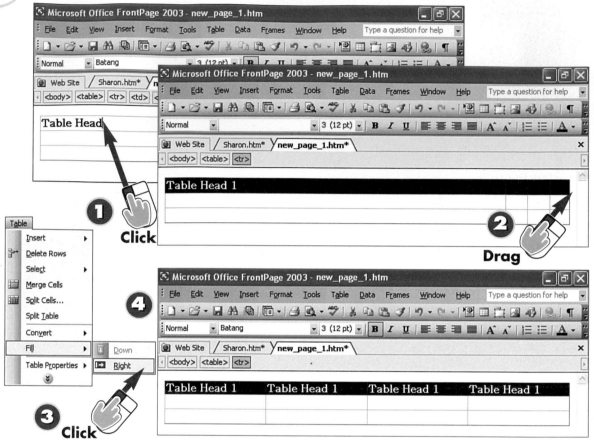

1 To fill a row, first click in the cell containing the content you want to add to other cells.

2 Drag to highlight the cell and the row.

3 Open the **Table** menu, choose **Fill**, and select **Right**.

4 The selected cells are filled with the contents of the first cell.

To save yourself the trouble of formatting the text or other contents of a whole table of cells individually, or when the contents of whole rows or columns of cells are similar or the same, you can save time with FrontPage's Fill tool, which automatically copies the contents of a cell (formatting and all) to other cells.

Use Fill to Make Column Heads

The Fill tool is a good way to create formatted column heads. Create and format one column head and then fill the rest of the row. When you type the other column heads, they'll automatically be formatted like the first one.

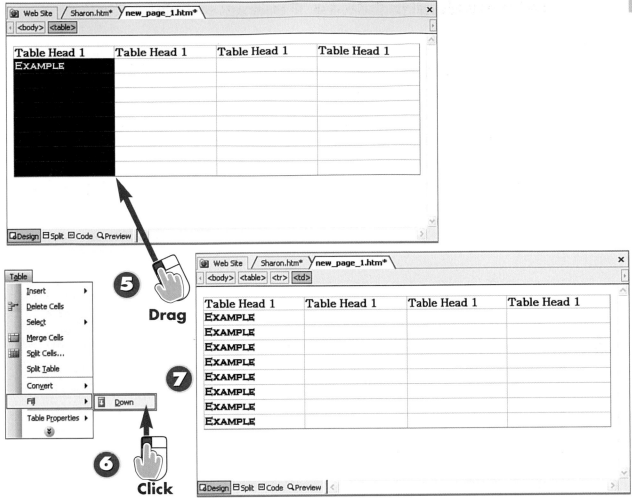

5 To fill a column, click in the cell containing the content you want to add to other cells. Drag to highlight the cell and the column.

6 Open the **Table** menu, choose **Fill**, and select **Down**.

7 The selected cells are filled with the contents of the first cell.

End

Fill Works for Any Kind of Content
You can use the Fill tool for any table contents—even pictures. All the contents, and all the formatting—image size, cell background, font, and so on—are copied to the other cells.

Using a Big Table to Design a Page

Start

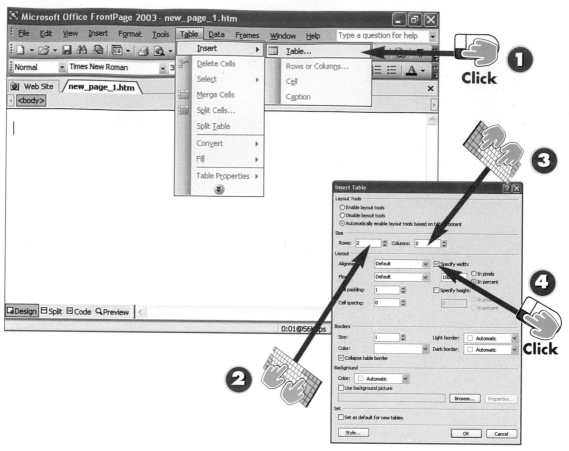

1 In a new blank page, open the **Table** menu, choose **Insert**, and select **Table**.

2 In the **Rows** field, type the number of rows the table should contain.

3 In the **Columns** field, type the number of columns the table should contain.

4 Click the **Specify width** check box to select it.

By creating a table so big that it covers the whole page, you give yourself the ability to put each chunk of page content—a paragraph here, a picture there—in its own cell. That enables you to arrange text and pictures in ways that would otherwise be impossible (unless you opted for "absolute positioning" and the limitations that come with it).

Some Tables Format Whole Template Pages
Most of the pages you create from templates are formatted by big tables. Use the table editing steps you learn in this Part to change the layout of pages you create from templates.

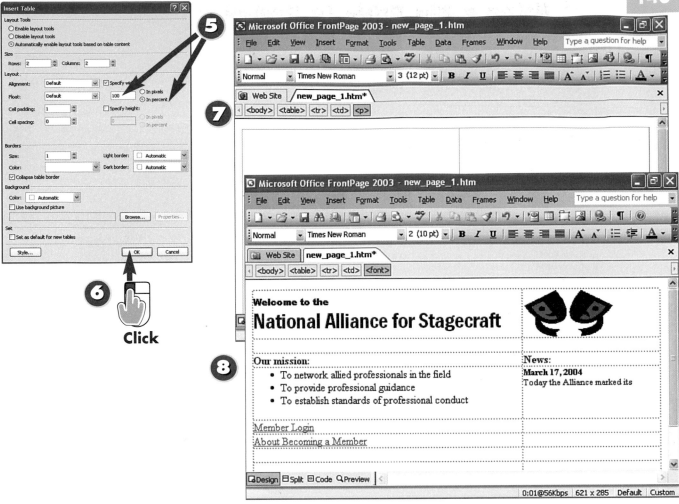

Click

5 Make sure that the number in the box is **100** and that the **In percent** option is selected, to create a table that is 100% the width of the page.

6 Click **OK** or press **Enter**.

7 A table with the number of rows and columns you specified is added to the page. Add content to the cells as needed.

8 Text and objects on your page appear where you place them.

End

Don't Worry If You Can't See the Whole Table Dialog Box
The Insert Table dialog box is very large; depending on the screen resolution you use on your computer, you might not be able to see the bottom of it, even if you drag it as high as you can. For now, don't worry—everything you need is near the top of the dialog box, except the OK button. If you can't see the OK button, remember that pressing the **Enter** key does the same thing as clicking OK.

Adding a Caption to a Table

Start

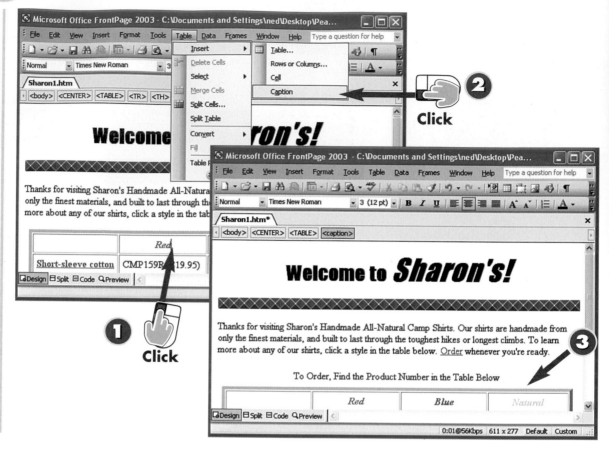

2
Click

1
Click

3

End

1 Click anywhere in the table to which you want to add a caption.

2 Open the **Table** menu, choose **Insert**, and select **Caption**.

3 Type your caption.

HINT

Double-Click to Format Your Caption
To format the text of the caption, double-click the caption to select it, and then apply formatting—font, size, color, and so on.

Dressing Up Tables with Gridlines

Start

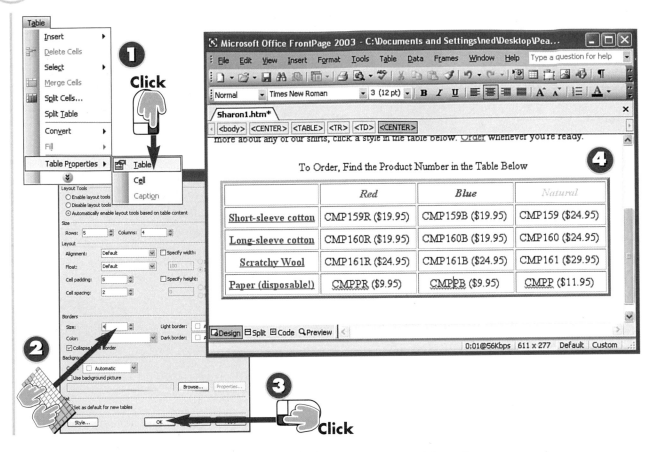

① After clicking anywhere in the table to which you want to add gridlines, open the Table menu, choose Table Properties, and select Table.

② The Table Properties dialog box opens. In the Borders area, click in the Size box and type a number for the width of the borders.

③ Click OK or press Enter.

④ Gridlines are added to the table.

End

So far, your table does a great job of lining up its content in rows and columns. But unless you've added them, the table lacks the nice grid of lines—and box all around—that delineate the content and can make the table look sharp.

A Bigger Border Size Makes a Thicker Border
In step 2, the higher the number, the thicker the border. Typing a **4** in the **Size** field creates a nice, moderately heavy border; typing **1** creates an elegant, thin border.

Cell Padding
Raising the number in the **Cell padding** field in the Table Properties dialog box creates more space around the cell contents, making the cells seem less crowded.

Choosing Custom Border Colors

Start

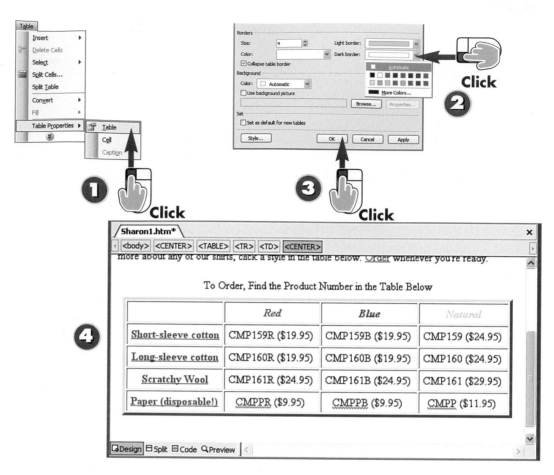

Click

Click

Click

1 Click anywhere in the table whose borders or gridlines you want to alter. Open the **Table** menu, choose **Table Properties**, and select **Table**.

2 In the **Borders** section of the Table Properties dialog box, choose a color from each of the three lists: **Color**, **Light border**, and **Dark border**.

3 Click **OK** or press **Enter**.

4 FrontPage applies your color selections.

End

INTRODUCTION

A table border or gridline is not one line, but three lines used together to create a 3D effect: a basic border line, a "light border" (a highlight), and a "dark border" (a shadow). You can pick the color for each part of the border.

TIP

Use "Apply" to Play with Table Choices
To experiment with the Table Properties dialog box, make any changes in the dialog box and then click the **Apply** button rather than OK. The changes are made, but the Table Properties dialog box remains open, so you can try different settings without having to reopen it.

Choosing a Background for a Table

Start

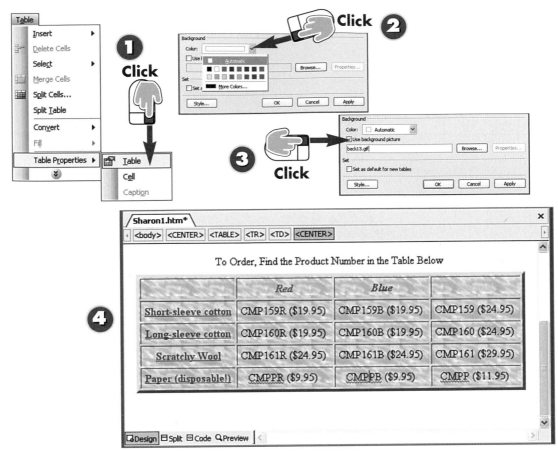

Click ①

Click ②

Click ③

④

Sharon1.htm*

`<body>` `<CENTER>` `<TABLE>` `<TR>` `<TD>` `<CENTER>`

To Order, Find the Product Number in the Table Below

	Red	Blue	
Short-sleeve cotton	CMP159R ($19.95)	CMP159B ($19.95)	CMP159 ($24.95)
Long-sleeve cotton	CMP160R ($19.95)	CMP160B ($19.95)	CMP160 ($24.95)
Scratchy Wool	CMP161R ($24.95)	CMP161B ($24.95)	CMP161 ($29.95)
Paper (disposable!)	CMPPR ($9.95)	CMPPB ($9.95)	CMPP ($11.95)

Design ⊟Split ⊞Code ⚲Preview

① Click anywhere in the table whose background color you want to change. Open the **Table** menu, choose **Table Properties**, and select **Table**.

② The Table Properties dialog box opens. To add a solid-color background to the table, open the **Color** list in the **Background** area and choose a color.

③ To add a picture background, click the **Use background picture** check box. Type the name of the picture file, or click **Browse**. When you're finished, click **OK**.

④ The selected background is applied.

End

INTRODUCTION

Unless you add a background to a table, the page's background color or image shows through the table (but does not obscure the table's content or borders). But a table can have its own background, different from that of the page, to make the table—and more importantly, its contents—really stand out.

HINT

Background Picture Trumps Background Color
If you choose both a background image and a background color, the color is irrelevant—a background image overrides a background color.

Adding New Rows

Start

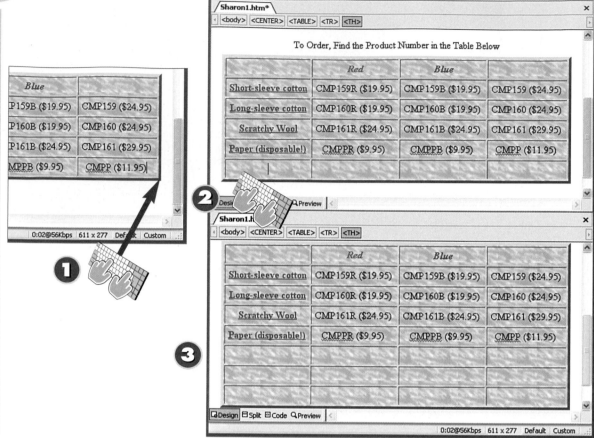

1 In the bottom row of the table, click in the cell farthest to the right, and press the **Tab** key on your keyboard to create a new row.

2 A new row is added. To add even more rows, keep pressing **Tab**.

3 More rows are added, one for each time you pressed the Tab key.

End

Ooops.... The table needs another row. No need to start over; just add what you need to the bottom of the table.

TIP

Insert a Row Anywhere in a Table
To insert a new row, but not at the bottom, click in any cell in the row you want to be directly *above* the new row. Then, open the **Table** menu, choose **Insert**, and select **Row or Columns**; then click **OK** in the dialog box that appears.

Adding New Columns

Start

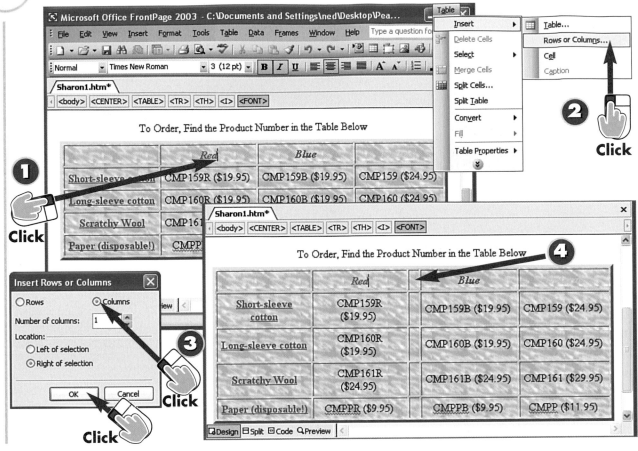

1 Click in any cell in the column that will be to the left of the new column.

2 Open the **Table** menu, choose **Insert**, and select **Rows or Columns**.

3 Click the **Columns** option, and click **OK**.

4 A new column is added.

End

INTRODUCTION

Ooops, redux! Suppose that your table needs another *column.* Fortunately, adding one is simple.

TIP

Add Multiple Columns
To add more than one column to the right of the selected column, change the setting in the **Number of columns** field in the **Insert Rows or Columns** dialog box.

TIP

Adding a Left Column
If you want the new column to be the leftmost column, click in the column that's farthest left and perform steps 2 and 3, but click the **Left of selection** option before clicking **OK**.

Fine-Tuning Row and Column Sizes

Start

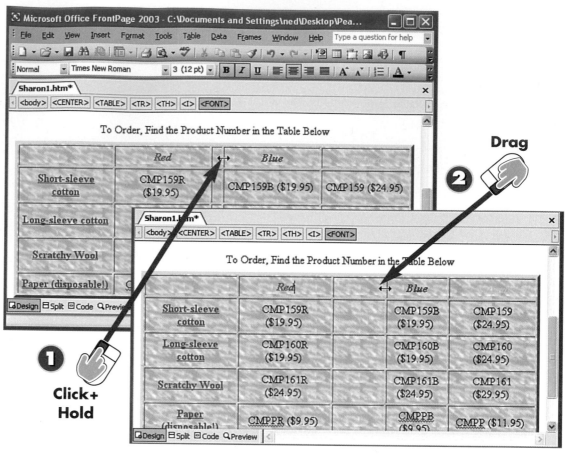

Drag
2

1
**Click+
Hold**

End

1 Using your mouse, point to the border of the row or column you want to resize. When the pointer becomes a two-sided arrow, click and hold.

2 Drag the row or column border until the row or column is the size you want it to be, and then release the mouse button.

PART 8

INTRODUCTION

After you insert all your content into the table, you might want to fine-tune the width of columns or height of rows—especially when you're using a table to control page layout. You can do this simply by dragging the space between two rows or columns.

TIP

Making All Rows and Columns the Same Size
To make all rows or all columns the same size, regardless of their contents, open the **Table** menu and then choose **Distribute Rows Evenly** or **Distribute Columns Evenly**.

TIP

Undoing Your Fine-Tuning
If you're not happy with your fine-tuning, you can make the table revert to basing its row heights and column widths on the size of cell contents by clicking anywhere in the table, opening the **Table** menu, and choosing **Autofit**.

Aligning a Table on the Page

Start

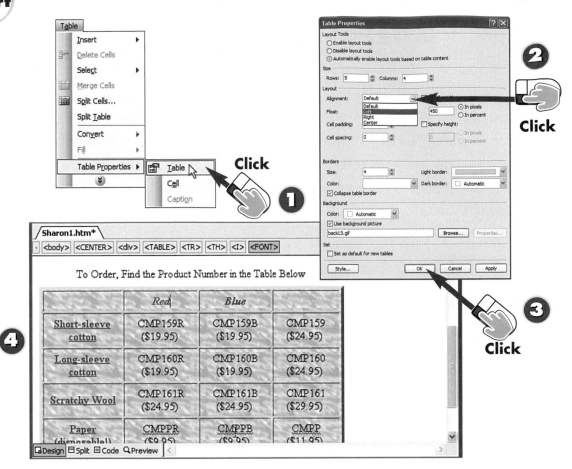

Click

Click

Click

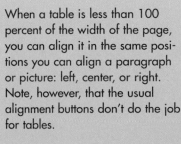
4

1 After you've clicked anywhere in the table you want to align, open the **Table** menu, choose **Table Properties**, and select **Table**.

2 The Table Properties dialog box opens. Click the **down arrow** next to the **Alignment** field and choose **Left**, **Center**, or **Right** from the list that appears.

3 Click **OK** or press **Enter**.

4 The table is aligned.

End

When a table is less than 100 percent of the width of the page, you can align it in the same positions you can align a paragraph or picture: left, center, or right. Note, however, that the usual alignment buttons don't do the job for tables.

Building a Web Site

In FrontPage 2003, you can easily create a set of pages, insert hyperlinks in each that lead to the other pages, and publish them as a site—you needn't fuss with FrontPage's Web sites. Creating Web sites, however, has its advantages. For example, when you apply a theme (refer to Part 2), you'll have the option of applying the theme to the whole site, giving the pages in that site a consistent appearance—and avoiding the effort of changing them one by one. Likewise, when you run the spell-checker, you'll see an option to check all pages in the Web site at once.

Best of all, a FrontPage Web site enables you to add *link bars* to your pages— that is, rows of buttons or text links that lead to other pages in the site. When you use FrontPage link bars, you don't need to create the hyperlinks behind them—that's automatic. And when you change a page's title, the link bar buttons leading to that page from other pages change automatically to the new title.

FrontPage's Web sites aren't essential. But they can save you a lot of time.

Web Site in Navigation View

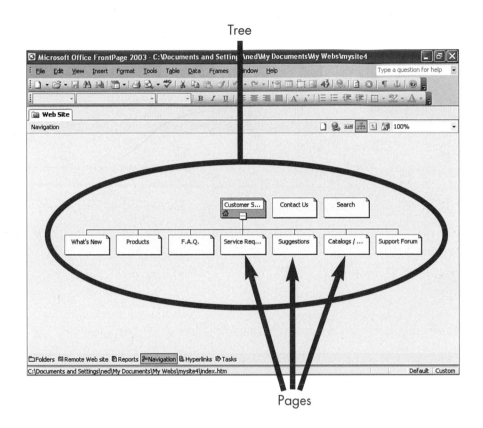

Starting a New Web Site with a Wizard

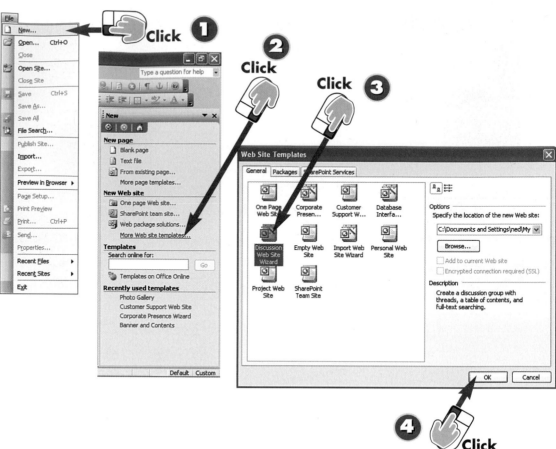

1 Open the **File** menu and choose **New**.

2 The New task pane opens. In the **Other templates** section, click the **More Web site templates** link.

3 The Web Site Templates dialog box opens. Click each wizard icon (the ones with magic wands) in the General tab, and read the description that appears on the right.

4 When the description shown is the best available match for the site you want to create, click **OK**.

The quickest and easiest way to kick off a new site is to use a wizard. The wizard builds a rough site (built on a template) that shows the general organization and feel you're going for; you can then edit that site in any way you want to make it your own.

TIP

Choosing Where to Save Your Site
Between steps 3 and 4, you can enter a disk location in the **Options** box to choose where the new Web site will be saved. That'll save you time when you save the site later.

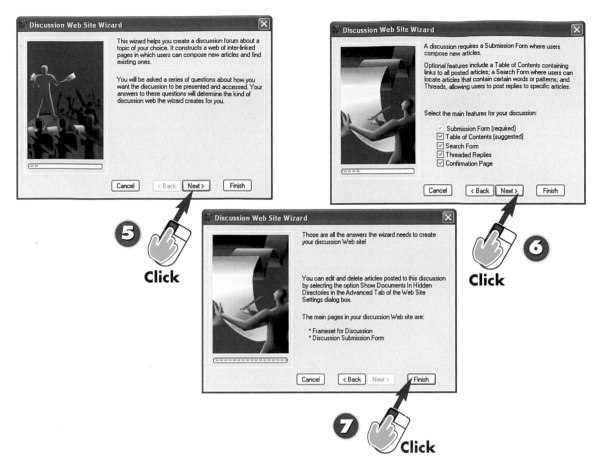

5 FrontPage launches the selected wizard. Read the wizard's Welcome message, and then click **Next**.

6 Work through the wizard screens presented to you, making any changes you want and clicking **Next** to proceed to the next screen.

7 On the wizard's final screen (where the Next button is no longer an option), click **Finish** to create the Web site.

End

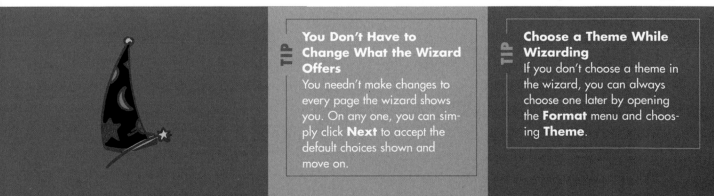

TIP

You Don't Have to Change What the Wizard Offers
You needn't make changes to every page the wizard shows you. On any one, you can simply click **Next** to accept the default choices shown and move on.

TIP

Choose a Theme While Wizarding
If you don't choose a theme in the wizard, you can always choose one later by opening the **Format** menu and choosing **Theme**.

Navigating Your Web Site

Start

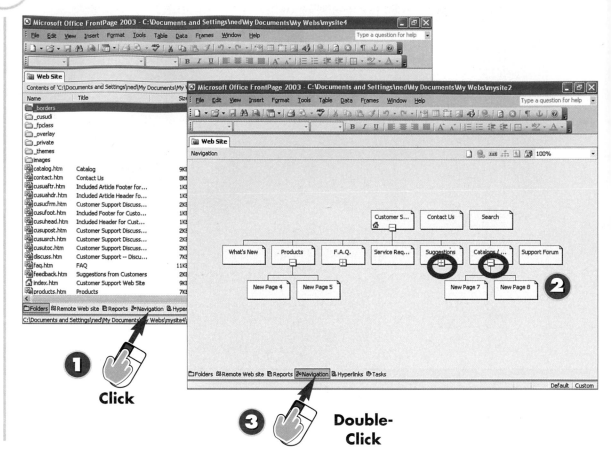

Click

Double-Click

End

1 In the **Views** bar, click the **Navigation** button.

2 The Web site is displayed in Navigation view. To show or hide page icons in branches of the tree, click the **plus** or **minus** icons.

3 To view and edit any page in the Web site in Design view, double-click the page's icon in Navigation view.

Right after you create a Web site with a wizard, you might find yourself in Tasks view. Tasks are really only important for dividing work among multiple authors creating a site together. For now, you need to switch to Navigation view, which displays the pages in the Web site in a tree diagram.

The Tree Does Not Show All

The apparent relationships among pages in the tree do not necessarily reflect the way pages are linked together. However, these relationships are important, because they can determine which pages the link bar on a given page points to. (See the tasks "Changing the Link Bar," "Adding a Link Bar," and "Testing a Link Bar" later in this part for more information.)

Seeing All of the Tree

Start

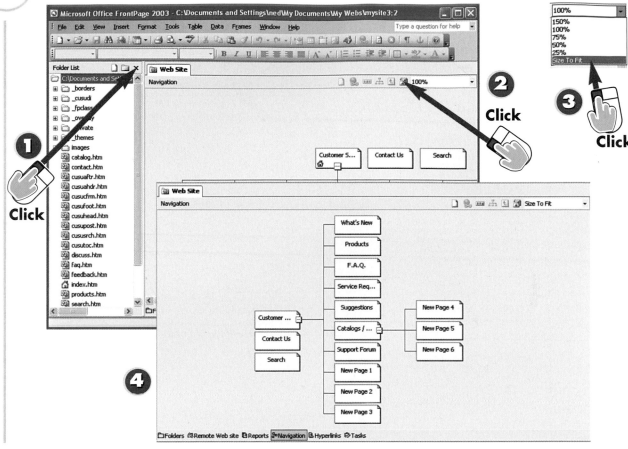

Click

2 **Click**

3 **Click**

4

1 If the folder list or the task pane are open, hide them by clicking the Close (x) button in the upper-right corner of each.

2 On the Navigation toolbar, click the **Portrait/Landscape** button to change the presentation of the tree from horizontal to vertical, or vice versa.

3 If steps 1 and 2 don't do the job, click the **down arrow** next to the Zoom field on the Navigation toolbar and choose **Size to Fit**.

4 The icons representing the pages in the Web site are resized to fit in the window.

End

TIP

Focusing on One Branch of the Tree
Sometimes you need to focus your attention on just one branch, or *sub-tree*, of the site. To display only one subtree in Navigation view, click the page icon of the subtree you want to view, and then click the **View Subtree Only** button on the Navigation toolbar.

Closing and Opening a Web Site

Start

Click ①

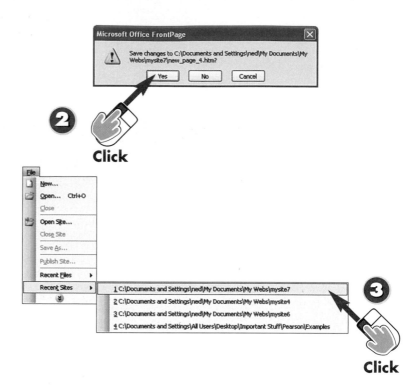

Click ②

Click ③

① To close a Web site, open the **File** menu and choose **Close Site** or simply exit FrontPage.

② If any pages in the site have been changed but not saved, a message appears, asking whether you want to save changes. Click **Yes** to save.

③ To open a Web site, open the **File** menu, choose **Recent Sites**, and then choose the site you want.

End

It's not necessary to save Web sites—changes to a Web site are saved automatically as you create and edit it. However, pages you change within the site must be saved. You can save pages as you work on them or just save when you close or exit, as shown in the following steps.

TIP

Opening a Web Site You Haven't Seen in a While
To open a Web site you haven't edited lately, open the **File** menu and choose **Open Site** to open the Open dialog box. Open the folder containing the site you want to open, click the desired site to select it, and click the **Open** button.

Adding a Page to a Web Site

Start

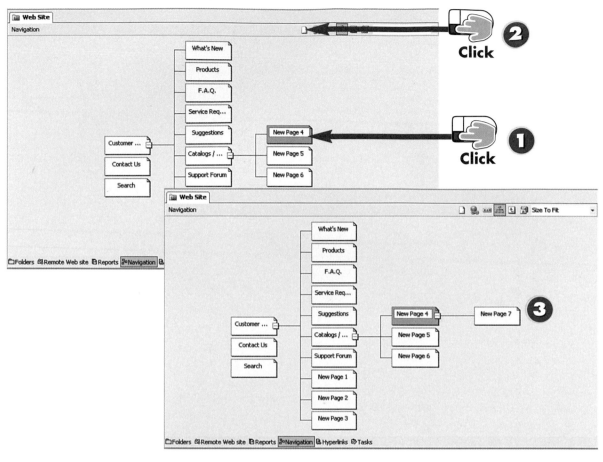

Click ② ①

Click

③

1. In Navigation view, click the page in the tree that is directly above where you want the new one to appear in the site.

2. Click the **New Page** button on the Navigation toolbar.

3. A new page is added as a subtree of the selected page.

End

INTRODUCTION

After your site is built, you might find you are short a page or two. Before you start editing individual pages, it's best to go ahead and add the remaining pages you need to complete the site.

HINT

Site Theme Is Added Automatically to New Pages

If your Web site has a theme applied to it, the theme is automatically applied to any new page you add.

Deleting a Page from a Web Site

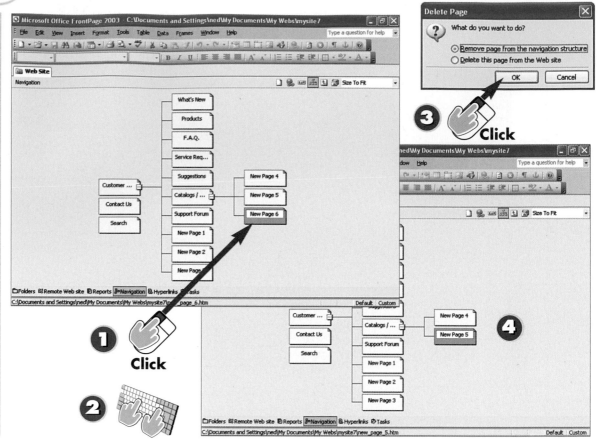

1 In Navigation view, click the page you want to delete.

2 Press the **Delete** key on your keyboard.

3 Choose whether to remove the page from the link bars of other pages in the site (but leave the page file in place) or to delete the page file altogether, and then click **OK**.

4 The page is deleted from the site.

HINT

FrontPage Helps You Avoid Deleting Pages You Might Want to Keep

If the page you delete has other pages under it, FrontPage asks in step 2 whether you want the page *and all pages below it* deleted, or simply removed from all link bars.

Moving a Page

Start

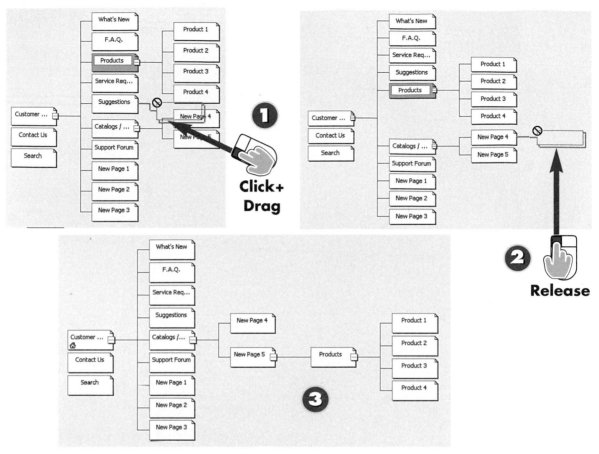

1 Click+ Drag

2 Release

3

1 Click and drag the page to where you want it to go, watching carefully for the line that appears to show how the page would relate to those around it.

2 When the line shows the relationship you want, release the mouse button.

3 The page—and all pages directly below it in the tree—are moved.

End

TIP

Use Undo to Undo Page Additions, Deletions
Anytime you add, delete, or move a page in a site, you can click the **Undo** button to reverse that action prior to saving. After you save the site, the changes remain.

Changing the Link Bar

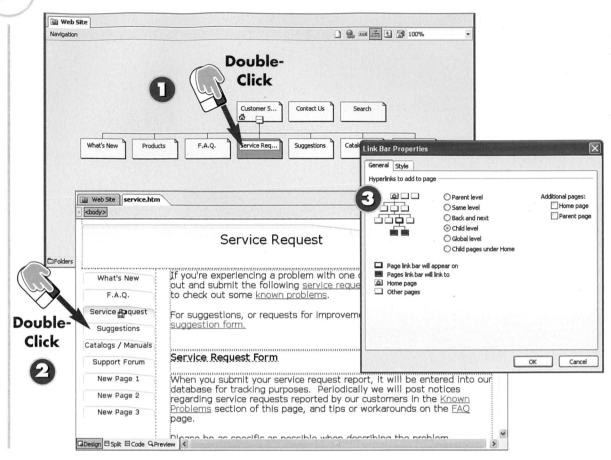

1 In Navigation view, double-click the page whose link bar you want to modify.

2 The page you selected opens in Design view. Double-click the link bar.

3 The Link Bar Properties dialog box opens. Examine the diagram of the Web site and the key beneath it. As you make changes in the dialog box, the diagram shows the results.

INTRODUCTION

Most Web site templates add a link bar to each page automatically. Although you might want to keep the bar, you might prefer that any given page include a different set of buttons or show different formatting than what the template gives it. Here's how to change the bar on any page.

TIP

Deleting a Link Bar
To delete a link bar, click it once to highlight it and then press the **Delete** key on your keyboard. Note that you must remove the bars one page at a time; you cannot remove it from a whole Web site at once.

HINT

To Change the Link Bar, Change the Theme
If your site uses a theme (see Part 2), you can change the appearance of the link bar buttons by changing the theme.

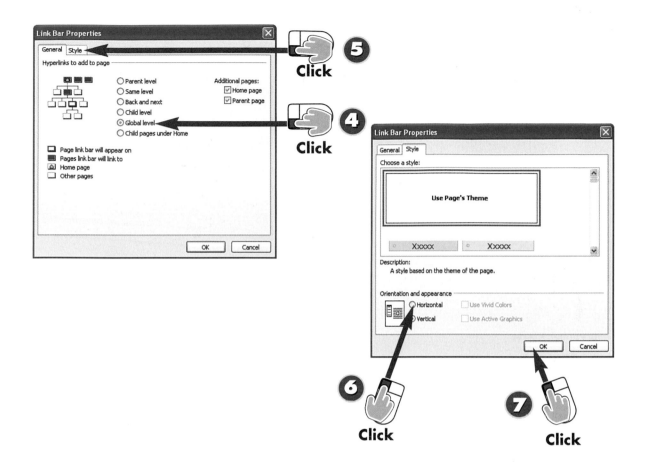

Click

Click

Click

Click

4 Choose which set of pages the bar should have links for, such as **Parent level** (the row directly above, in the same branch), **Child level** (the row below), and so on.

5 Click the **Style** tab.

6 Choose the bar's orientation and appearance: as a **Horizontal** row or **Vertical** column, and as **Buttons** or simple **Text** links.

7 Click **OK** and the link bar is altered according to the selections you made.

End

HINT

Adding a Home or Parent Page to a Link Bar
In a link bar, you can optionally add the Web site's home page or the page's parent page (the page directly above it in its subtree) by checking the check boxes provided.

TIP

Back and Next Gives You Link Buttons Forward and Ahead
The **Back and next** option does not link the link bar to specific pages. Instead, it creates a bar with two buttons, which—when clicked by a person who visits your site—have exactly the same effect as clicking the browser's **Back** and **Forward** buttons.

Adding a Link Bar

Start

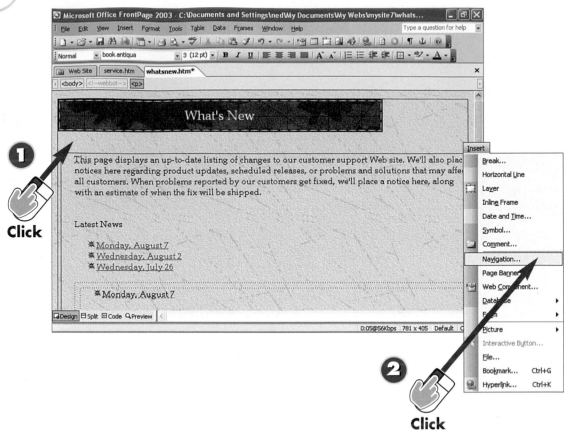

Click

Click

① Viewing the page in Design view, click where you want to insert the bar.

② Open the **Insert** menu and choose **Navigation**.

INTRODUCTION

Most, but not all, Web site templates add a link bar automatically. If you don't have one for your site and you want one, this task shows you how to add it.

HINT

Moving a Link Bar
You can move a link bar by clicking it and dragging, just as you would move a picture.

Click

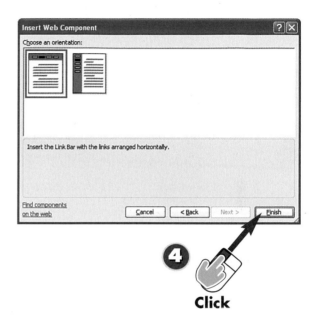

Click

3 The Insert Web Component dialog box opens. Click **Link Bars** in the Component type list, click a link bar in the **Choose a bar type** list, and click **Next**.

4 FrontPage leads you through the remaining steps for formatting and creating the type of bar you've chosen. Click **Next** after each step, and then click **Finish** on the final screen.

End

Link Bars Work Only in Web Sites

HINT

You can add link bars only to pages within a site. Individual pages created outside a Web site cannot use this feature—although you can, of course, create a bar of links on your own, using the steps in Parts 5 and 6.

PART 10

Adding Cool Effects

Most of the important cool stuff you can add to pages has been covered already, especially in Parts 6 and 7. But there are a few other fun doodads FrontPage 2003 can add to your pages—at a price.

The cool stuff you can add by following steps in this part falls mostly into a category called *components*. In some cases, components in Web pages show up properly only when the page is viewed through Internet Explorer 4 or later, not through other browsers. (This also means that you must have Internet Explorer 4 or later installed on your computer to preview your work!) In other cases, a component supports multiple browsers but requires that special Microsoft software—called *FrontPage Extensions*—be installed on the server where the page is published.

So although the stuff in this part is fun and easy to add, you should refrain from using it, except in pages to be published on a local intranet where all users have Internet Explorer 4 or later, or where you know that the FrontPage Extensions are on the server. On the Internet, too many of your potential visitors will be unable to see your masterpiece in its full glory.

Inserting Web Components

Insert Web component

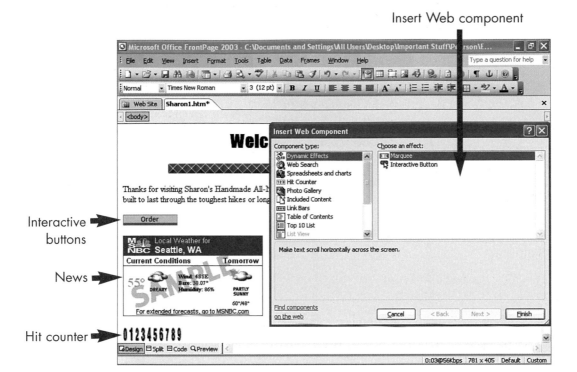

Creating Interactive Buttons

Start

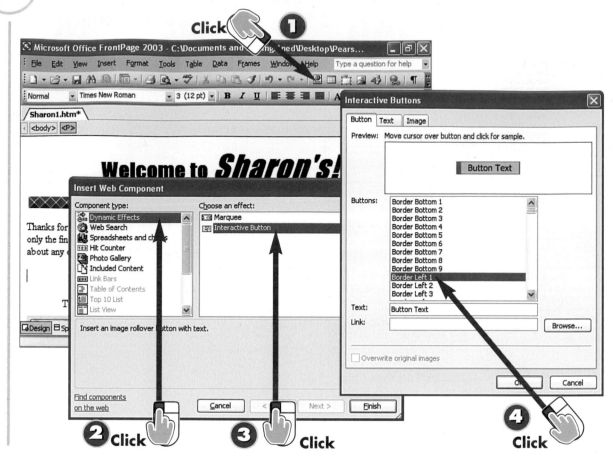

Click ①

②Click

③ Click

④ Click

① In Page view, after you've clicked on the Web page in the spot where you want the button to appear, click the **Web Component** button on the Standard toolbar.

② The Insert Web Component dialog box opens. Click the **Dynamic Effects** option in the **Component type** list.

③ Click the **Interactive Button** option in the **Choose an effect** list, and click **Finish**.

④ The Interactive Buttons dialog box opens. In the **Buttons** list, click a button type and preview it in the Preview area.

TIP

Preview to See Your Interactive Buttons Work
To see your interactive buttons in action, you must save the page and then preview it in the **Preview** tab or in a Java-compatible browser (Internet Explorer 4 or later or Netscape Navigator 4 or later).

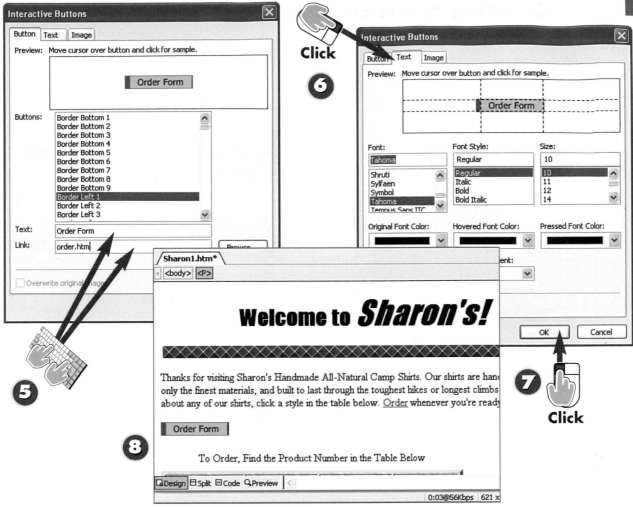

5 In the **Text** box, type the text you want to appear on the button and type the file-name or URL the button should lead to in the **Link** box.

6 Optionally, you can change the settings in the **Text** and **Image** tabs of the Interactive Buttons dialog box to further customize your button.

7 Click **OK**.

8 The button is added to your page.

TIP
Double-Click a Button to Change It
To change the effect or other settings for a button, double-click the button to display the Interactive Button dialog box, make your changes, and click **OK**.

TIP
Reshape/Size Buttons Just Like Pictures
Change the size, shape, or position of an interactive button by performing the same steps you use to change the size, shape, or position of a picture (see Part 6).

Counting Visits to Your Site

Start

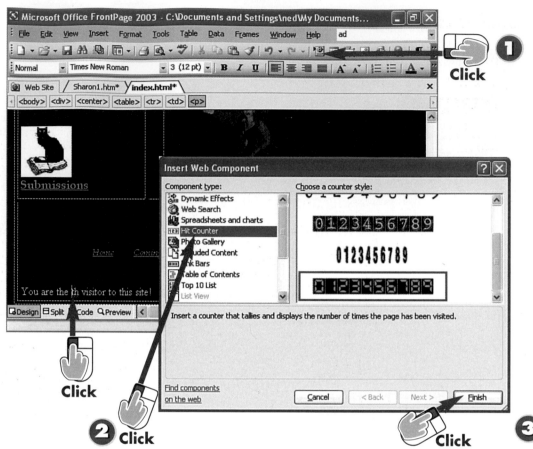

1 In Page view, after you've clicked on the Web page in the spot where you want the counter to appear, click the **Web Component** button on the Standard toolbar.

2 The Insert Web Component dialog box opens. Click the **Hit Counter** option in the **Component type** list.

3 Click a **Counter Style** and click **Finish**.

INTRODUCTION

On your online travels, you've no doubt seen pages that proudly report that you are the "5056th visitor" to the site, or words to that effect. That little feature is called a *hit counter*, and it does more than tell your visitors how popular you are; it helps you track your traffic.

4 The Hit Counter Properties dialog box opens. Choose additional options, or just click **OK**.

5 The hit counter is added to your page.

End

See Your Hit Counter Work
To see your counter in action, publish your page on a server that's equipped with Microsoft's FrontPage Extensions. To learn whether a particular server is so equipped, talk to the system administrator.

Making a Text Marquee Scroll Across the Page

Start

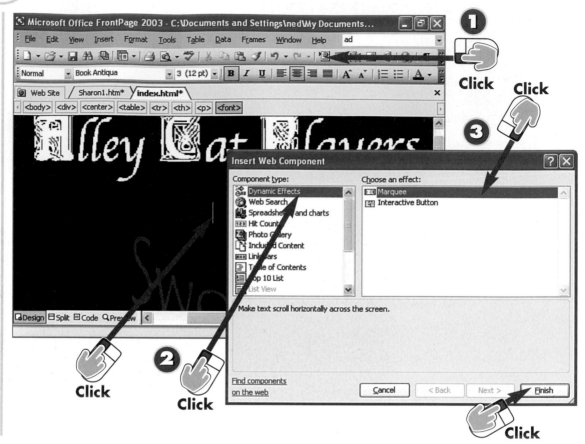

Click **Click**

Click **Click** **Click**

1. In Page view, after you've clicked on the Web page in the spot where you want the marquee to appear, click the **Web Component** button on the Standard toolbar.

2. The Insert Web Component dialog box opens. Click the **Dynamic Effects** option in the **Component type** list.

3. Click the **Marquee** option in the **Choose an effect** list, and click **Finish**.

TIP

Scrolling Marquees Don't Work in Netscape
At this writing, scrolling marquees are supported *only* in Internet Explorer—not in any other browser. Navigator users will see your marquee's text as regular, static text on the page. However, marquees do not require FrontPage Extensions.

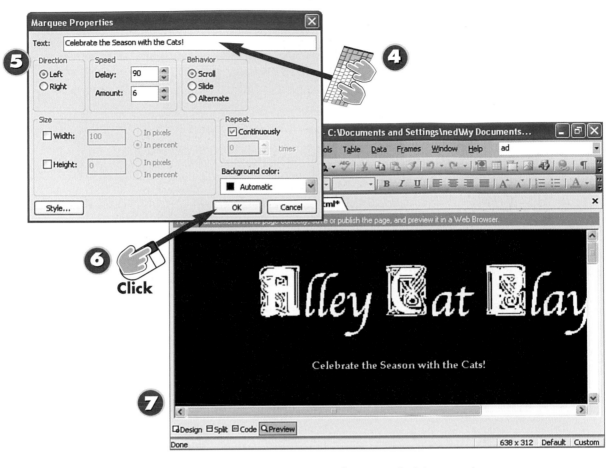

Click

4. The Marquee Properties dialog box opens. In the **Text** field, type the text you want to scroll across the page.

5. If you want, make changes to the **Direction**, **Speed**, **Behavior**, and other settings.

6. Click **OK**.

7. The marquee text is added to your page. To view it in action, click the **Preview** button. The marquee text scrolls across the page in the manner you specified.

Double-Click a Marquee to Change It

TIP

To change the options or text for a scrolling marquee, just double-click the marquee to open the **Marquee Properties** box, change whatever you want, and then click **OK**.

Adding News and Other Content That Updates Automatically

Start

Click **1** Click

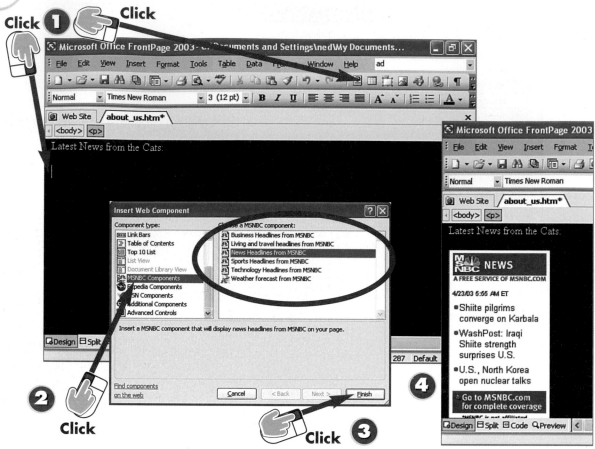

2 Click

3 Click

4

1 In Page view, after you've clicked on the Web page in the spot where you want to add news or other content, click the **Web Component** button on the Standard toolbar.

2 The Insert Web Component dialog box opens. In the **Component type** list, click the type of content you want to add to your page.

3 The list on the right side of the Insert Web Component dialog box changes depending on your selection in step 2. Choose an option and click **Finish**.

4 The content is added to your page.

End

INTRODUCTION

FrontPage 2003 gives you an easy way to add to your pages the latest news headlines, maps, stock quotes, and more. Once in your pages and online, this information is updated automatically as news changes. It's a great way to add value to your site and to encourage visitors to stop by often.

TIP

You Have a Variety of "News" Options
In step 2, instead of choosing MSNBC Components for news, you can choose MSN Components to add stock quotes or a Web search box, or choose Expedia Components to add a map.

Inserting a Date and Time Field

Start

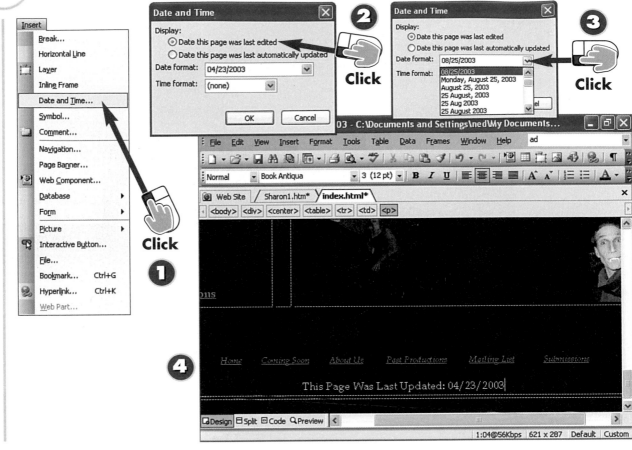

Click

1. In Page view, after you've clicked on the Web page in the spot where you want the date and/or time to appear, open the **Insert** menu and choose **Date and Time**.

2. The Date and Time dialog box opens. In the Display area, click an option, depending on your needs.

3. Click the **down arrows** next to the **Date format** and **Time format** fields and choose the date/time format you want to use. Then click **OK**.

4. The field is added to your page.

End

Adding Page Transitions

Start

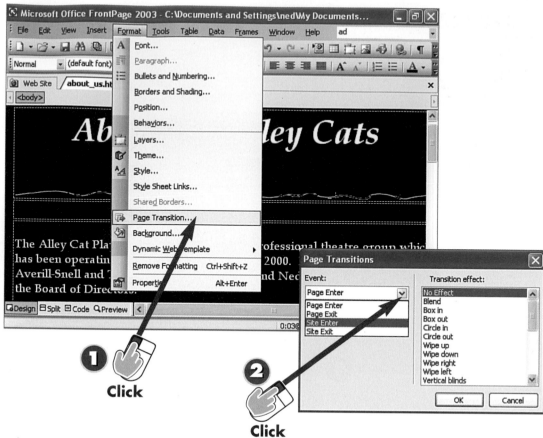

Click

Click

1. After you've displayed the Web page to which you want to add a transition in Page view, open the **Format** menu and choose **Page Transition**.

2. The Page Transitions dialog box opens. Click the **down arrow** next to the **Event** field and choose when the transition should occur.

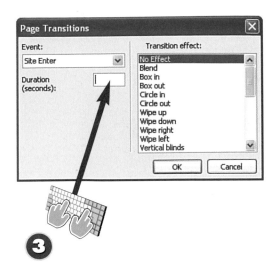

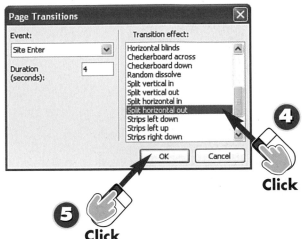

Click

Click

3 In the **Duration** field, type the number of seconds the effect should last. (From 2 to 5 seconds is a good ballpark figure.)

4 Under **Transition effect**, choose the effect you want.

5 Click **OK**.

End

TIP

Preview to See Page Transitions

To see your page transition in action, you must save the page and then preview it in a Java-compatible browser such as Internet Explorer 4 or later or Netscape Navigator 4 or later.

Adding Fill-in-the-Blanks Forms

A *form* is a part of a Web page that collects information from your visitors by prompting them to select options from lists, check boxes, and to use other such *form fields*. When finished supplying information, the visitor clicks a Submit button to send the data to the server to be processed.

Creating the part of a form you see is easy—in fact, some of the templates include ready-made forms. But the part you see is only half the form; the other half is the *script*, a behind-the-scenes program for collecting and processing the data that visitors enter.

How you handle the script depends on how the server where you will publish your page is equipped (see Part 12 for more information). If the server is equipped with Microsoft software such as *FrontPage Extensions* or *Windows SharePoint Services*, you can forget about the script and configure the form processing from within FrontPage. If not, you'll need a programmer to create a script for you.

This part shows how to add the visible parts of a form to your Web page and gets you started on dealing with the processing. I recommend that you consult closely with the administrator of the server where you will publish to set up the processing of your form.

Building a Form

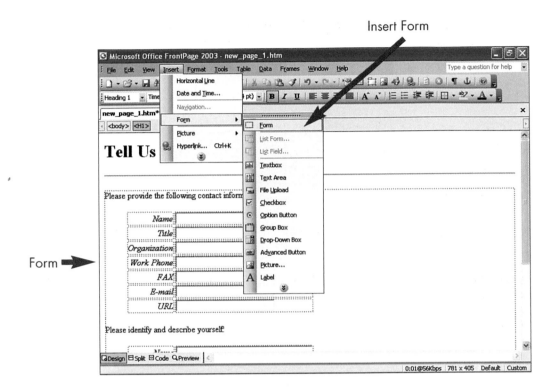

Insert Form

Form

Running the Form Page Wizard

Start

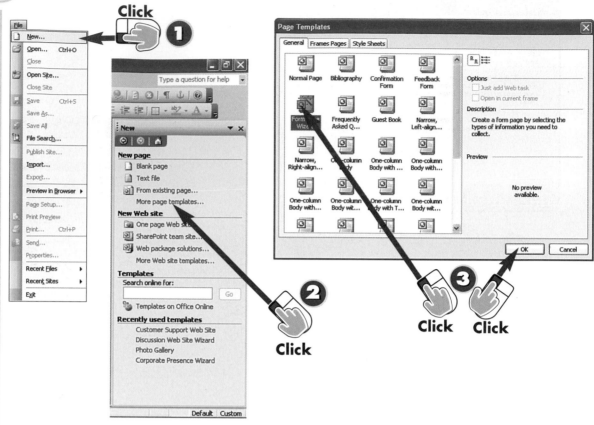

Click

1

Click

2

Click **3**

Click **Click**

---

1 Open the **File** menu and choose **New** to open the New task pane.

2 In the **New Page** area of the New task pane, click the **More Page templates** link.

3 The Page Templates dialog box opens. In the **General** tab, click the **Form Page Wizard** icon, and then click **OK**.

You can add a form to any page (as you learn to do in the next task, "Starting a New Form from Scratch"), or you can create a new page that already has the form in it. A great way to do that is to run FrontPage's Form Page Wizard, which custom builds a form page based on answers you give to simple questions.

HINT

Some Templates Already Have Forms
You could also create a form page by using a page template that already has a form in it. Page templates that have their own forms include Guest Book, Feedback Form, and Confirmation Form; the Corporate Presence Wizard (see Part 9) also includes forms.

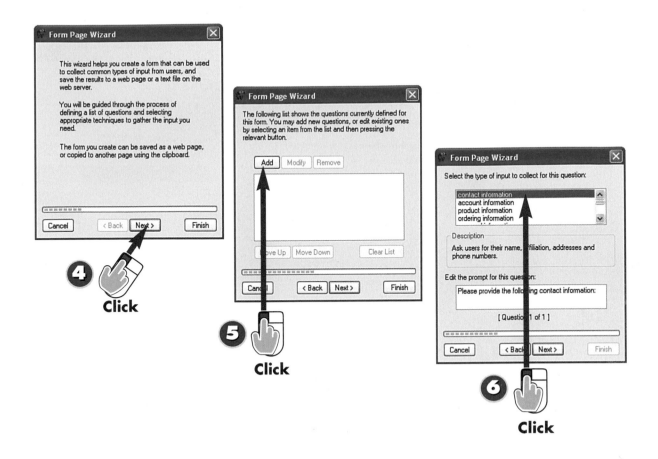

4 FrontPage launches the Form Page Wizard. Read the information in the first screen and click **Next**.

5 Forms gather information from site visitors by asking the visitors certain questions. To begin selecting the questions that will appear on your form, click the **Add** button.

6 Click an option in the **Select the type of input to collect for this question** list. A description of the selected option appears in the **Description** area.

Label Now or Later

When choosing each type of information to collect, you can change the prompt label that FrontPage will attach to the part of the form you selected by changing the text in the box at the bottom of the dialog box. You can also edit this label later, in your page.

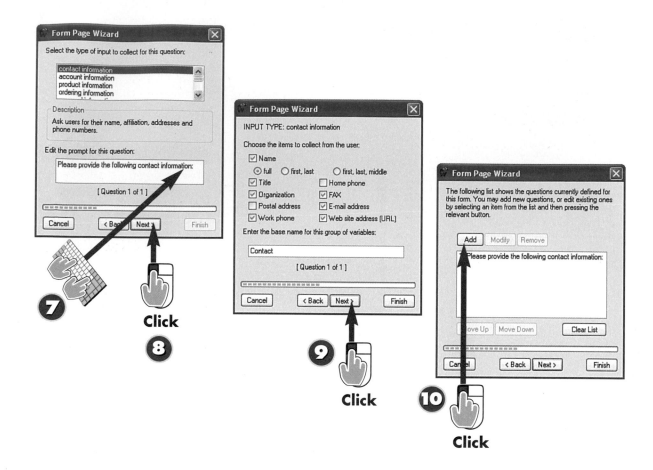

7 FrontPage suggests a way of wording the question. To change the wording, type over the suggested wording in the **Edit the prompt for this question** field.

8 Click **Next**.

9 Choose from any options presented (they vary depending on your selection in step 6), clicking **Next** to advance to the next screen.

10 Repeat steps 5–9 for each question you want to add to your form.

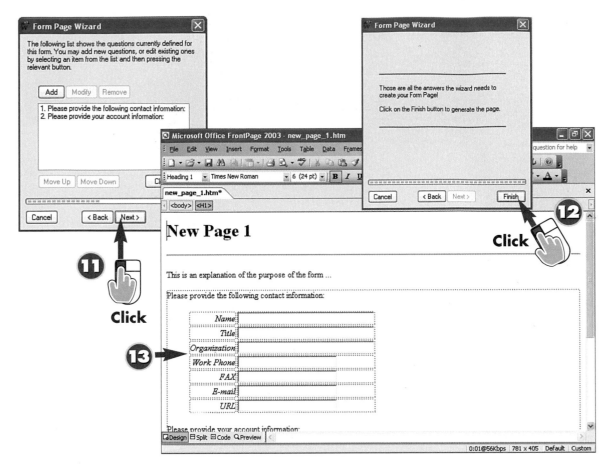

11 When you finish adding questions to your form, click **Next** to choose general form options.

12 When the wizard reports that it has no more questions to ask you, click the **Finish** button.

13 FrontPage creates a page with a form containing the questions you added.

End

The remaining steps help you arrange and format the questions you've selected into a form that's right for your site, and—more importantly—help you decide what FrontPage should do with the information it collects from your visitors.

Play Around with Wizards

This task demonstrates only one of the many different types of forms you can create by making different choices in the Form Page Wizard. Feel free to experiment. If you don't like the results, it's easy to start over.

Starting a New Form from Scratch

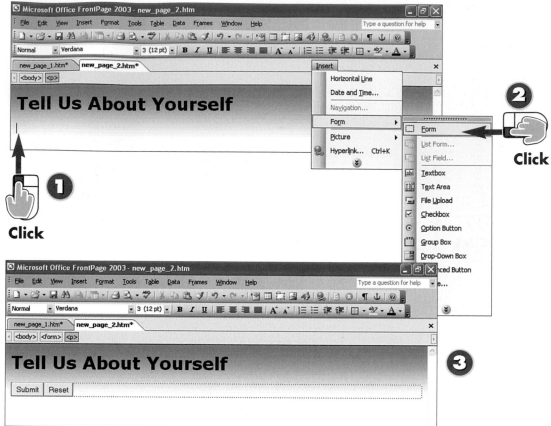

Click

Click

1. In Design view, click in your page where you want the form to appear.

2. Open the **Insert** menu, choose **Form**, and select **Form**.

3. A form containing Submit and Reset buttons is placed on the page.

Form Boxes Expand to Meet Your Needs
Don't worry about the size of the form box. It will expand automatically to hold whatever fields you put in it (covered in the next several tasks).

Adding Form Fields

Start

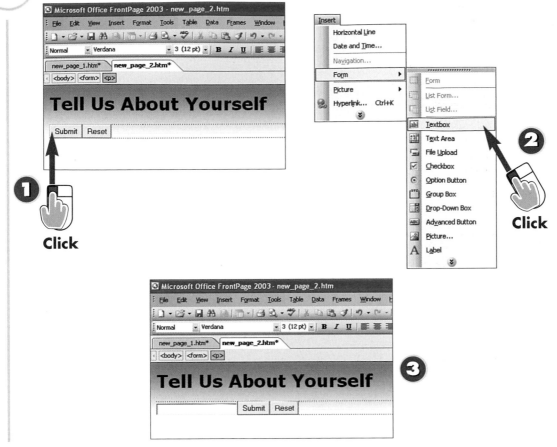

Click

Click

End

① Click just to the left of the Submit button to place the insertion point there.

② Open the **Insert** menu, choose **Form**, and select any of the field types shown (here, Textbox is selected). The field is inserted.

③ To insert a second field to the right of the first, repeat step 2. To insert a new field beneath the first, press **Enter** to start a new line, and then repeat step 2.

After you've inserted an empty form with Submit and Reset buttons on a page, you can begin adding the *form fields*—that is, the text boxes, lists, and other fields a visitor uses to enter information or select options. Each type of field features different options, but inserting basic fields is pretty much the same all around.

Fields Can Go Anywhere
You can insert your fields above, below, or even beside the Submit and Reset buttons, but most page authors place those buttons at the very bottom of the form.

Choose Field Types Carefully
If you want a short typed response, use a one-line text box field; use a text area field for longer responses. Option buttons and check boxes let visitors choose one or more options shown.

Labeling Form Fields

Start

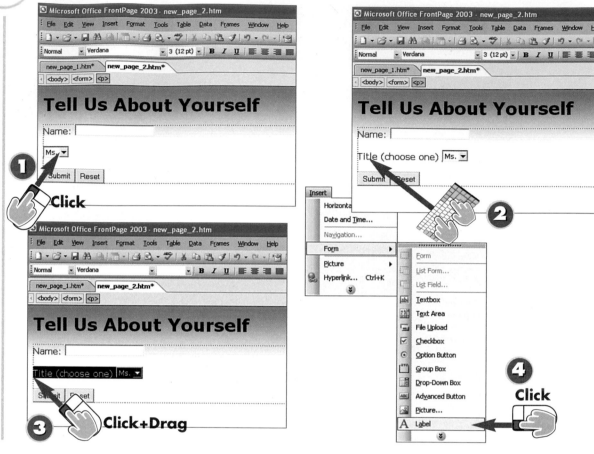

① Click next to the field to which you want to add a label to place the insertion point there.

② Type the label text.

③ To connect the label to its associated field, click and drag to select both the label and its field.

④ Open the **Insert** menu, choose **Form**, and select **Label**.

End

Of course, each form field needs an onscreen name or label so that the visitor will know what type of data to enter in it. After you create a label, you will associate it to the field it represents.

Labels Can Take Text Formatting

After you create the label, you can select it and apply to it any character formatting (font, bold, and so on) you want.

Put Your Labels Anywhere You Want

You can place the label anywhere you want in relation to the field (above, to the left, to the right, or below), as long as no other label or field comes between a label and its associated field.

Adding Options to a Drop-Down Box

Start

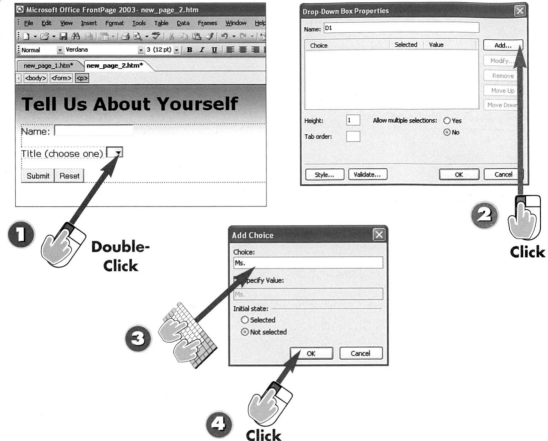

Double-Click

Click

Click

1 In your form, double-click the drop-down box field.

2 The Drop-Down Box Properties dialog box opens. To add the first option, click the **Add** button.

3 The Add Choice dialog box opens. In the **Choice** field, type the item text.

4 Click **OK**.

Drop-down boxes are different from most other fields in that they contain a list of options from which the site visitor can select. That means you must populate each list box you create with your own set of options.

You Can Allow Your Visitors to Make Multiple Selections in a List

In the Drop-Down Properties dialog box, note that you can click the **Yes** option button in the **Allow multiple selections** area to permit visitors to make multiple selections from one list. Using that option might confuse visitors accustomed to lists that permit one choice only. When you want to allow multiple selections, it's better to show option buttons or check boxes.

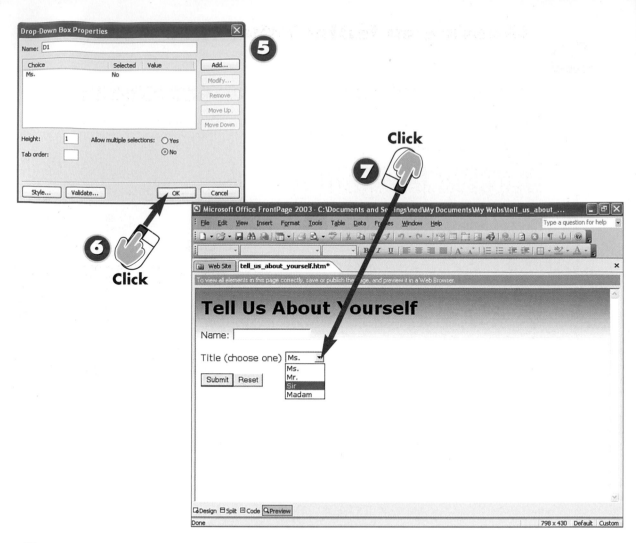

5 Repeat steps 2–4 to add more options to the drop-down box.

6 When you finish adding options to the drop-down box, click **OK**.

7 Click the drop-down box's **down arrow** to display the options you entered.

End

Rearranging List Items
You can rearrange the order of items in the list by using the Drop-Down Box Properties dialog box. To do so, click an item whose place in the order you want to change, and then click the **Move Up** or **Move Down** button.

Choosing an Initial Value for a Field

Start

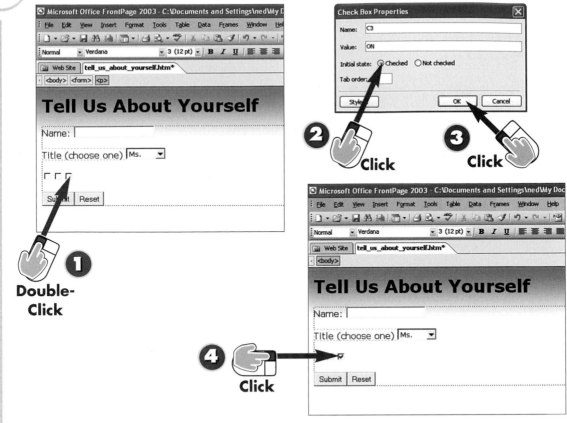

Double-Click ①

② **Click**

③ **Click**

④ **Click**

① Double-click the field for which you want to choose an initial value. The field's Properties dialog box opens. (In this example, it's the Check Box Properties dialog box.)

② In the **Initial value** field or the **Initial state** field (depending on the field type), type or select the initial value or state.

③ Click **OK**.

④ The field on the form is updated to contain the initial value or state you specified.

End

An *initial value* or *initial state* is an optional default form entry you offer your visitors to save them time. For example, if you predict that most visitors will probably choose a particular check box or menu item, you can make that option appear to be preselected on the form. If the visitor disagrees, she can always change that entry.

Setting an Initial Value for a Drop-Down List
To set the initial value for a drop-down box, double-click the field on the form. Double-click an option to open the Modify Choice dialog box; then, in the **Initial state** area, click the **Selected** option.

Leave Some Fields Alone, at First
Most other fields you see in the Properties dialog boxes—such as **Name** and **Value**—are related to processing the form data. It's best to leave these fields alone, or to change them only in consultation with an expert.

Changing the Size and Shape of Fields

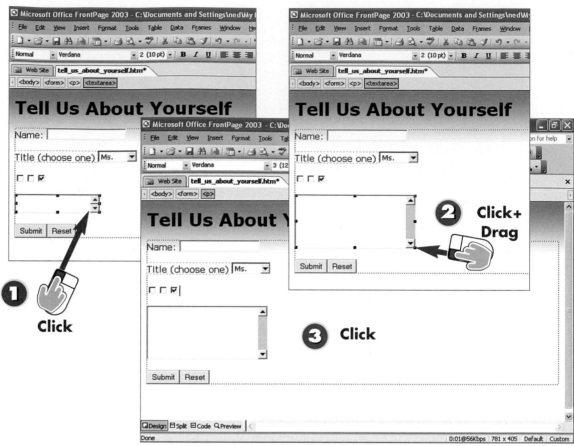

Start

Click

1

2 Click+ Drag

3 Click

End

1 Click the field you want to modify to select it.

2 Click one of the sizing handles that appear around the field and drag to change the field's size or shape, just as you would a picture.

3 Click anywhere outside the field to deselect it.

TIP

Use Handles to Resize Text Boxes
For a scrolling text box, you can drag the top, bottom, side, or corner handles to change the size and/or shape of the box. You can change the width of a one-line text box, but not its height; conversely, you can change a menu's height, but not its width. Option buttons and check boxes cannot be resized or reshaped.

Choosing How a Form Is to Be Processed

Start

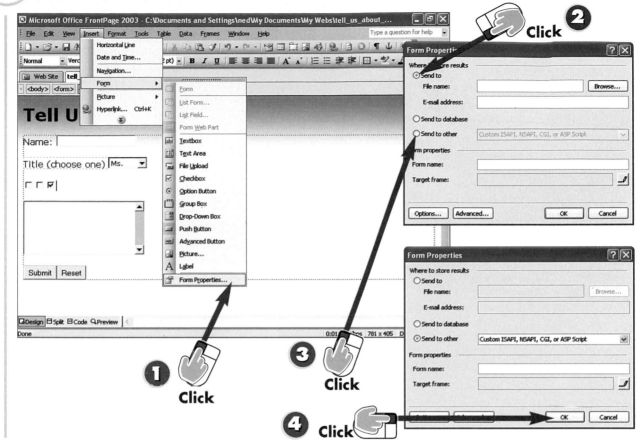

Click **2**

Click **3**

Click **1**

Click **4**

1. Click anywhere in the form. Then, open the **Insert** menu, choose **Form**, and select **Form Properties**. The Form Properties dialog box opens.

2. If your server uses FrontPage Extensions, click **Send to** and, in the **File name** field, specify the name and location of the file where data received from visitors will be stored.

3. If the server *does not* have FrontPage Extensions, click **Send to other**, and consult with the system administrator about having a script written.

4. Click **OK**.

End

You must work closely with your Internet service provider or the administrator of the server where you will publish your pages to set up form processing. Before you begin, it is imperative that you contact your server administrator and ask whether the server on which your form will be published has FrontPage Extensions installed.

Locating the File
If you don't know the exact location of the file where form data will be stored, click the **Browse** button next to the **File name** field in step 3 to locate the file.

You Can Send Data As an Email Message
When the server has FrontPage Extensions, you can optionally enter an email address in step 2. All form responses will be sent automatically to that address as email messages.

Publishing Your Page Online

A play is not lines on a page. Even after it's written and printed, it does not officially become a play until an audience sees it on stage.

The same goes for a Web page. It's not really a Web page until it gets on the Web (or at least onto your school's or company's local intranet, if that's your page's destination). In this part, you find places on the Web where you can put your pages and FrontPage Web sites, and then learn how to publish them.

To follow the same analogy of a play, you are never quite sure of the performance until you read the reviews. By the same token, FrontPage 2003 provides various report tools that can help you keep your site running smoothly.

Preparing to Publish

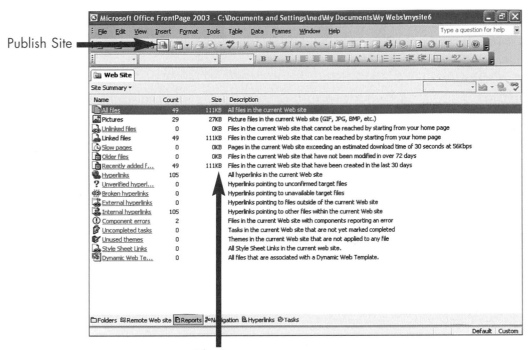

Publish Site

File Sizes

Checking Out File Sizes and Performance

Start

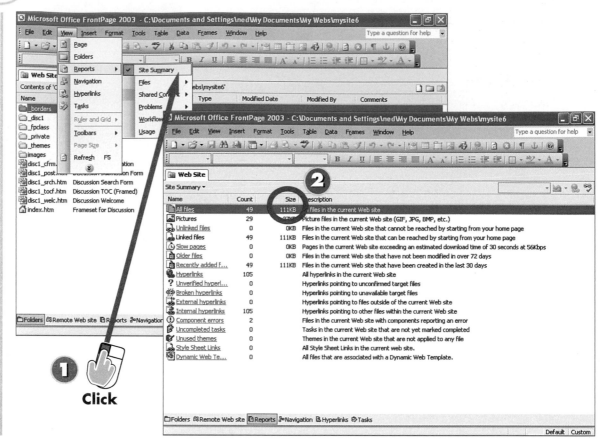

1 After you open the page or Web site whose size and performance you want to examine, open the **View** menu, choose **Reports**, and select **Site Summary**.

2 At the top of the **Size** column, you'll see the total number of kilobytes in the current page or Web site.

FrontPage can display or print a variety of useful reports, most of which are designed to help manage large multi-author projects. But a few can help you determine the size and potential performance of your pages before publishing, so you can make adjustments if necessary.

Finding the Fattest Files
If the size of the site appears excessive, open the **View** menu, choose **Reports**, and select **All Files**. Then, open and edit the largest files, paying particular attention to removing or reducing pictures (including picture backgrounds).

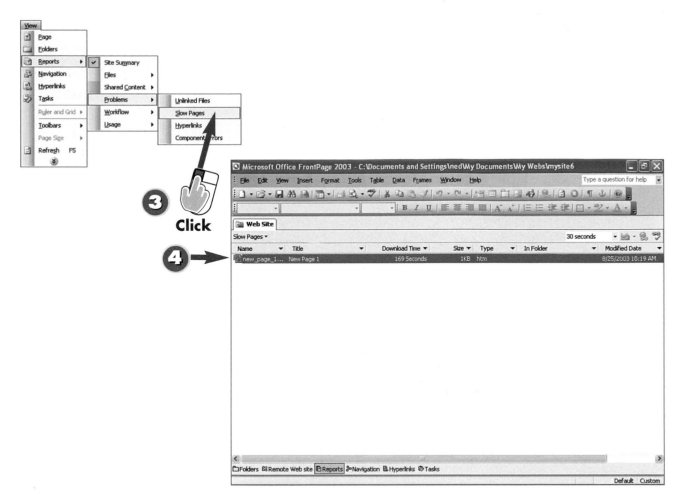

Click

3 Open the **View** menu, choose **Reports**, select **Problems**, and click **Slow Pages**.

4 FrontPage lists any pages that will take longer than 30 seconds to appear online at the speed of your Internet connection.

End

Performance Estimates for a Page

While viewing any page in Page view, look in the lower-right corner of the FrontPage window to see an estimate of how long that page will take to appear at the speed of your Internet connection.

Finding Space on a Web Server

Start

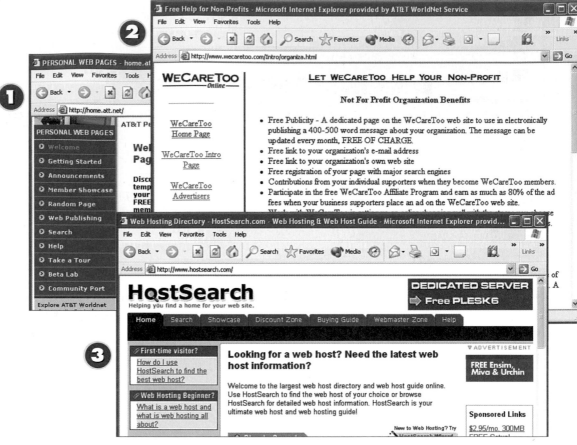

1 Check your Internet service provider's Web site to see whether you're entitled to some space on its server.

2 Use a search engine (such as Yahoo!) to search for Web pages that contain the terms **Web hosting** or **server space** to find companies offering space.

3 Visit HostSearch (**www.hostsearch.com**), a Web site that helps you search for Web space providers.

INTRODUCTION

Before they can be seen by others, your pages must first be stored on the hard drive of a Web server (or intranet server) of a Web host. Your first step is finding some server space where you will be permitted to put your pages. The following are some good ways to find that space.

There's Free Space Out There!

If you search Yahoo! or another search tool for **free Web hosting** or **free server space**, you might find companies offering free space, usually to nonprofit or other worthy organizations.

Try Your Company or School Server

If your page is business- or school-related, you might find that you can publish it free on your company's or school's Web site. Contact the administrator of that site.

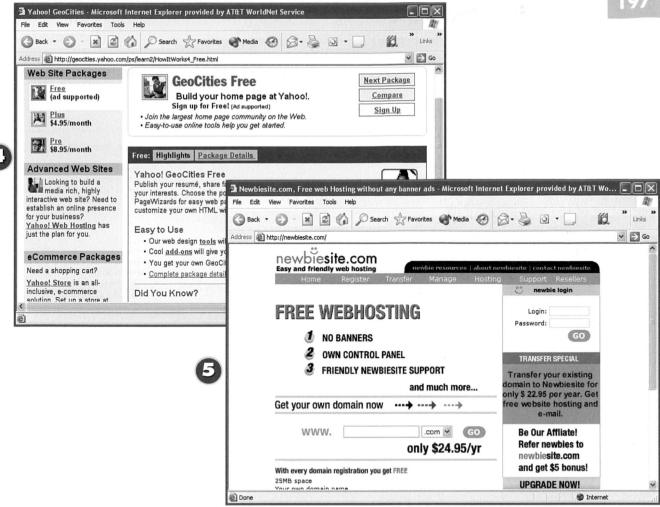

4 Check out the various online communities, such as Yahoo!'s GeoCities (**geocities.yahoo.com**), which offer free server space.

5 Newbiesite (**www.newbiesite.com**) offers a deal similar to GeoCities, but with a different selection of tools and options.

End

Some Free Space Has Strings Attached
Some online communities that offer free server space require that you "join" their online community first, include their ads on your pages, and follow some unusual procedures for publishing your pages.

How Much Space Do You Need?
A single Web page with text and a few pictures is usually smaller than 100KB (about 1/10th of a megabyte). A site of 10 or 12 different pages might easily fit in less than a megabyte of server space.

Getting Your Own Domain

Start

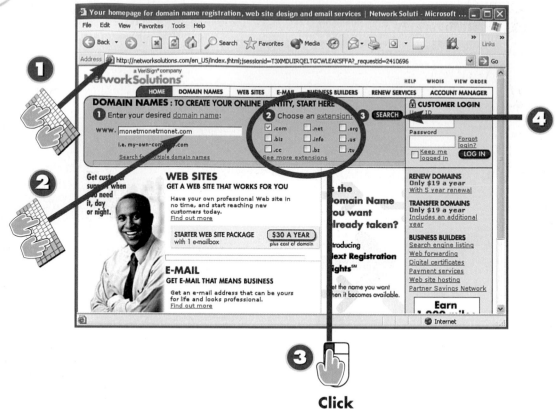

Click

1. Type **www.networksolutions.com** in your browser's **Address** area to visit the Network Solutions Web site.

2. In the first section of the page, type the domain name you want to use.

3. In the second section of the page, click the check box for the extension you want to use (see the tip on this page for more information about extensions). Here, **.com** is selected.

4. Click the **Search** button to determine whether the name you chose has already been registered by someone else.

If you simply take some space on someone else's server, your page will be accessible through the Web, but it won't have the sort of catchy Web address that gives you a Web identity, such as **www.buick.com**. Instead, your page's address will be expressed as a directory on that server. If you want your own Internet name, you need to purchase a domain.

Other Sources for Domain Registration
Network Solutions is not the only provider of domain names. To learn about other companies that can register your domain for you, do a Web search on **domain registration**.

End Your Domain Name
The final part of the domain name can be **.com** (commercial site), **.org** (organization), **.edu** (educational), **.net** (network), or any of a variety of newer options, such **.biz** (business). If you're not sure what to use, that usually makes you a **.com**.

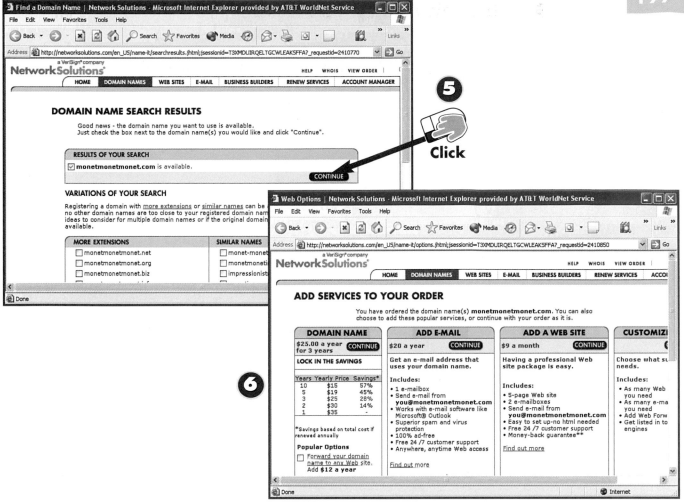

5 If no one else has registered the domain you chose, a screen tells you it's available. Click the **Continue** button to begin the process of buying the domain.

6 Follow the onscreen instructions to create and pay for your domain. When finished, contact your Web-hosting company to have your new domain set up on that company's server.

End

Domain Taken?
If, in the screen shown in step 5, Network Solutions displays a report detailing who owns the domain you had chosen for yourself, that means that the domain is taken. Return to step 2 and try a different domain name.

Your ISP May Register Your Domain for You
Most ISPs will register a domain for a setup fee of around $20. In addition to the setup fee, the ISP might collect an additional fee from you to pay a required registration fee.

Publishing from FrontPage

Start

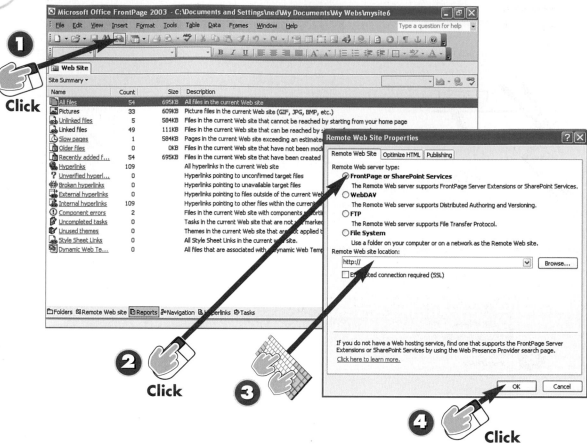

Click

① Click

② Click

③

④ Click

① After you open the page or Web site you want to publish, click the **Publish Site** button on the Standard toolbar. The Remote Web Site Properties dialog box opens.

② In the **Remote Web server type** area, click the option button for the type of publishing communication required by your Web-hosting company.

③ In the **Remote Web site location** field, type the address to which the page or Web site should be published.

④ Click **OK**.

INTRODUCTION

Most Web-hosting companies prefer that you *upload*—that is, publish your Web files from your PC to the Web server—by using an Internet tool called *FTP*. If you're familiar with FTP, you can do it that way. If you're not, FrontPage can *publish* your pages for you, as outlined here.

TIP

You Need to Be Online to Publish

If you are not connected to the Internet when you begin this task, FrontPage opens your connection after step 1.

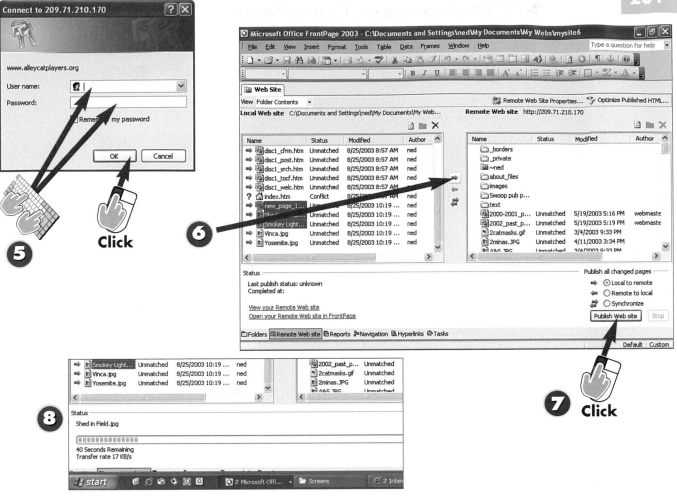

5 If the server prompts you, type your username and password (the ones provided by your Web-hosting company for publishing) and click **OK**.

6 The left pane contains the files in the current site. The right pane contains files on the remote Web site.

7 To upload only certain files to the remote site, select them in the left pane, and then click the → button. To publish all files in the current Web site, click the **Publish Web Site** button.

8 Watch the bottom of the dialog box as the wizard uploads your files.

End

Don't Worry About Copying New Over Old
Don't worry about copying new files on your PC over old files with the same name on the server. That's usually what you want to do—replace old with new.

After Publishing, Test Your Pages
After uploading, use your Web browser to go to the URL you typed in step 3 to see your new page online.

Updating and Editing Your Page

Start

Click

2

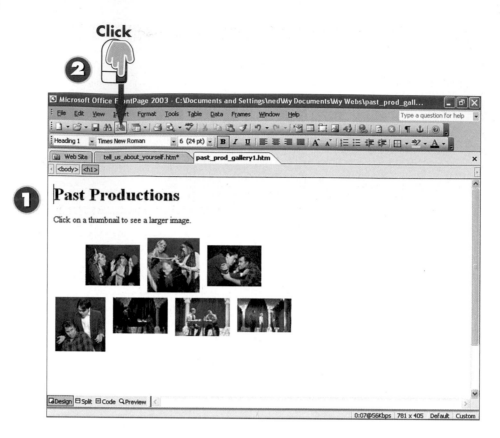

1 Edit your page or Web site as normal in FrontPage.

2 Click the **Publish Site** button on the **Standard** toolbar. Publishing happens automatically, based on the selections you made the first time you published.

End

Fixing or updating your pages after you publish them is easier than publishing them in the first place. You can't edit the copies of your pages stored on the Web server; instead, you simply make changes to the original files on your PC and publish again. The changed files automatically replace the old ones on the server.

TIP

Updating Is Even Easier Than Publishing
When you click the **Publish Site** button, FrontPage automatically reuses the settings you entered the first time you published your page or Web site. If you need to change those settings, open the **File** menu and choose **Publish Site**.

Checking Out Site-Submission Services

Start

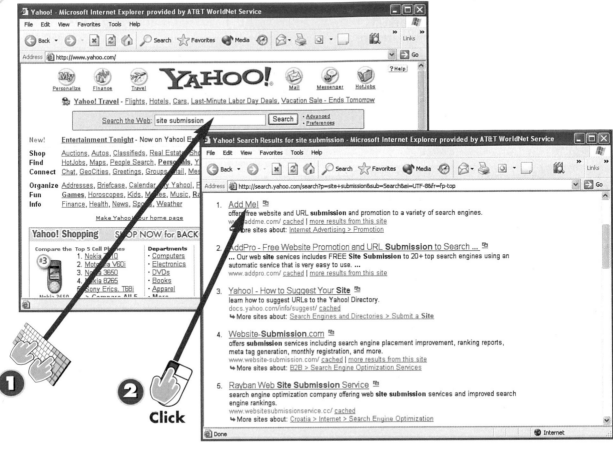

Click

① In the box at the top of the main Yahoo! page (**www.yahoo.com**), type **site submission** and click **Search**.

② In the search results, read the descriptions to find sites that offer site submission.

End

INTRODUCTION

You can promote your site effectively by simply adding it to one or two popular directories such as Yahoo!. But for faster Web saturation, you can use any one of a number of commercial site-submission services, sometimes also known as *Web promotion* firms, which will submit your site to all major search tools and other directories. There might be a fee for the service.

TIP

Site-Submission Services Offer Useful Advice

By browsing the Web sites of the site-submission services, you can often pick up useful tips—free—that can help you promote your site more effectively.

TIP

There's Software for Site-Submission, Too

There are also site-submission software packages that you can install on your PC. Check out a product called Submissions at **www.submissions.com**.

Glossary

A

absolute positioning   A technique, supported in *FrontPage 2003*, for positioning pictures and other objects in a Web page precisely where you want them; traditional HTML Web authoring enables you only to position such objects generally.

alignment   The way text, a picture, or a table is aligned on a page. Left-aligned objects line up to the left margin, right-aligned objects line up to the right margin, and centered objects are centered between the left and right margins.

anchor   See *bookmark*.

animated GIF   A special kind of *GIF* image file that plays as a brief animated clip when viewed through a *browser*.

B

background   A color or image that covers the entire area behind the text and pictures of a Web page.

bookmark   An invisible marker in a Web page that provides a spot to which a link can point, so that a link can take a visitor straight to a specific spot within a page. Bookmarks are also known as targets or anchors in some Web authoring programs.

browse   1) To wander around the *World Wide Web* portion of the Internet, viewing Web pages through a *browser*. Also known as *surfing* or *cruising*. 2) To preview in a *browser* a Web page you're editing in *FrontPage 2003*.

browser   A program, such as Microsoft Internet Explorer or Netscape Navigator, that enables you to view Web pages.

bulleted list   A list of items in which each item is preceded by a marker, a "bullet," or some other symbol character. See also *numbered list*.

C

cell   The individual boxes that make up a *table*. One cell appears at each intersection of one row and one column.

cell alignment   A type of table formatting that enables you to control where within a *cell* the contents of that cell are aligned: left, right, center.

CGI (Common Gateway Interface) One method for creating scripts that make some advanced Web page features work, such as *forms*.

character formatting   Formatting that changes the style of text characters, such as applying *fonts*, bold, or italic.

check box   A small square box used to select objects in a program or a Web page *form*. Clicking an empty check box inserts a check mark there, indicating that the object or option next to the check box is selected.

clip art   Graphics, photos, and sometimes other media (such as sound and video clips) published in collections for convenient use in creating Web pages and other publications. *FrontPage 2003* includes its own library of clip art.

Clip Gallery   A program built into *FrontPage 2003* (and other *Office 2003* programs) that enables you to locate and use files stored in the *clip art* library and to add new items to that library.

collapsible list   A *nested list* in which a *visitor* viewing the list through a *browser* can choose to display or hide ("collapse") nested list items by clicking the major list items.

component   An object in a Web page that carries out a programmed action; components include hit counters, *marquees*, and *form* fields.

crop   To trim off one or more sides of a picture to cut the picture down to only the part you want to show.

D

dialog box   A box that pops up in Windows programs to provide the options necessary for completing a particular task. Different tasks display different dialog boxes.

domain   The top-level name address of a computer on the Internet. A user's Internet address is made up of a username and a domain name. Every Web server has its own unique domain and can play host to other domains as well.

download   The act of copying information from a server computer to your computer. See also *upload*.

Dynamic HTML (DHTML)   A set of technologies, including style sheets and scripting languages such as JavaScript, that enable a Web page to include a variety of advanced interactive features and design. (DHTML features function only when the page is viewed through a DHTML-compatible browser.)

E-F

email address   The Internet address used by an email program to send email to a particular Internet user or service (webmaster@ or help@). The address is made up of a username, an @ sign, and a domain name (user@domainname).

FAQ file   Short for *Frequently Asked Questions file*. A computer document, often made available on the Internet, containing the answers to frequently asked questions about a particular topic or Web site.

folder list   A tree of folders and files displayed in *Navigation view* to help you see and work with the organization of a *FrontPage Web site*.

font   A particular style of text.

font size   The relative size in which text appears onscreen.

form   A part of a Web page in which users can type entries or make selections that are then collected and processed. Forms require either the *FrontPage Extensions* or a *script* on the server.

frames   Multiple panes in a browser window, each of which displays a different Web page file. Web authors design frames pages to enable visitors to use the frames together as a single, multidimensional Web page.

FrontPage 2003   A Web-page authoring and publishing program for Windows (2000 and XP versions) from Microsoft, sold by itself.

FrontPage Extensions   A set of programs that, when installed on a Web *server*, enable *forms* and some *components* in Web pages created in *FrontPage 2003* to perform their tasks without the aid of a *script*.

FrontPage Web site   A group of Web page files designed, edited, and managed in FrontPage to work together.

FTP   Short for *File Transfer Protocol*. The basic method for copying a file from one computer to another through the Internet. Often used for publishing Web page files by *uploading* them to a server.

G–H

GIF   A form of computer image file using the file extension .GIF, commonly used for *inline images* in Web pages.

handle   A small, square box that appears along the outlines of tables, pictures, and forms when these objects are selected in *FrontPage 2003's* Design view. You drag handles to perform actions that affect the size and shape of these objects.

heading   A short line of text, often set large and bold, that marks the start of a particular section of a document, such as a Web page.

highlight color   A transparent band of color laid over selected text in a Web page to call attention to the text.

horizontal line   In a Web page, a straight line that divides sections of the page horizontally. Also known as a horizontal rule.

hotspot   In *FrontPage 2003*, a region within the area of a picture in a Web page. Web authors may define multiple hotspots within a single picture, so that clicking different parts of the picture activates different links. Pictures with hotspots are known generally in Web parlance as *image maps*.

HTML (Hypertext Markup Language)   The document formatting language used to create Web pages. The files produced by Web authoring programs such as *FrontPage 2003* are HTML files.

hyperlink   See *link*.

image map   See *hotspot*.

indent   To shift a paragraph or other page contents to the right, away from the left margin.

inline image   A picture that appears within the layout of a Web page.

interactive button   A link button in a Web page that changes its appearance when a visitor points to it or passes the mouse pointer over it.

Internet   A large, loosely organized internetwork connecting universities, research institutions, governments, businesses, and other organizations so that they can exchange messages and share information.

Internet Explorer   A *browser* for the World Wide Web, created by Microsoft. Internet Explorer version 6 is built into Windows XP and available free for other systems.

intranet   An internal network in a company, school, or other organization that is based on Internet technologies so that using it is just like using a *browser* on the *World Wide Web*.

J–K

Java   A programming language that can be used to create applets—programs that run inside a Web *browser*.

JavaScript   A method for creating *scripts* that make some advanced Web page features work, such as *forms*.

JPEG   A form of image file, using the file extension .jpg (or .jpeg), commonly used for *inline images*, most often photos, in Web pages.

L

link   Short for *hyperlink*, an object in a Web page that takes the visitor to another page, downloads a file, or starts some other action.

link bar   A bar of links (typically buttons), a feature of *FrontPage Web sites* that enables the author to edit all the link bars in a Web site by changing just one of them.

link source   The part of a link that a visitor actually sees in a Web page and clicks to activate the link. (The other part of a link is the *URL*.) A link source can be some text, an *inline image*, or a *hotspot*.

list box   In a *dialog box* or Web page form, a small box with a downward-pointing arrow at its right end. Clicking the arrow opens a list of options the user can click to select one to appear in the box.

loop   To play a sound, video, or music clip repeatedly.

M

mailto link   A link in a Web page that, when clicked by a visitor, opens the visitor's email program and creates a new message pre-addressed to a particular person.

marquee   A line of text that repeatedly scrolls across part of a Web page, used as an attention-getting device.

menu   A list of choices on a computer screen. A user selects one choice to perform an action with a software program.

N–O

Navigation view   A version of the *FrontPage 2003* window displayed when the user clicks the Navigation button in the *Views bar*. Used for managing a *FrontPage Web site*.

Navigator   Sometimes called *Netscape*, a popular *browser*.

nested list   A multilevel *bulleted list* or *numbered list* in which some list items are indented to form sublists under the item above them, as in an outline.

Netscape   Short for Netscape Communications Corporation, a software company that developed and markets the Netscape *Navigator Web browser*. Some people casually refer to Navigator as "Netscape."

network   A set of computers interconnected so that they can communicate and share information. Connected networks together form an internetwork.

numbered list   A list of items in which each item is preceded by a number, and the numbers go up as the list goes down. See also *bulleted list*.

Office 2003   A suite of application programs from Microsoft, available in several versions.

P–R

page transition   An animated effect that plays when a visitor moves between two pages in a *FrontPage Web site* or exits or enters the site.

paragraph   Any block of text ending in a paragraph mark (¶).

paragraph break   The space between two paragraphs in which a hidden paragraph mark appears.

paragraph formatting   Text formatting, such as *paragraph styles* or *alignment*, that can be applied only to a whole paragraph or paragraphs, never to only selected characters within a paragraph, like *character formatting*.

paragraph style   The principal form of text formatting on a Web page. Paragraph styles include six levels of *headings*, a style for normal text, and several different styles for creating lists.

Photo gallery   A feature of *FrontPage 2003* that enables the author to easily create and update a page displaying a gallery of photo images.

position box   A feature of *Dynamic HTML* that enables a Web author to precisely position a picture or other object within the area of a Web page.

publish   General term for copying Web pages to a Web server so that they can be viewed by others on the Web. The final step of Web authoring.

S

script   A program written in *JavaScript*, VB Script, Perl, or another such language, that can be invoked from a Web page to perform a particular task, such as processing a *form*.

search engine   A program, such as Google, often accessed through a Web page, that provides a way to search for specific information.

selection   Text, a picture, or some other object that the author has highlighted so that the next action the author performs affects only the highlighted text, picture, or object.

server   A computer on a network, used to store information and "serve" it to other computers that contact it through the network. A Web server stores Web pages that it serves to the browsers that contact it through the Internet.

shareware   Software programs that users are permitted to acquire and evaluate for free. Shareware is different from freeware in that, if a person likes the shareware program and plans to use it on a regular basis, he or she is expected to send a fee to the programmer.

signature   A block of text on a Web page, usually near the bottom, that identifies the page's author or the *Webmaster*. Signatures often include a *mailto link* to the author's *email address*.

style   See *paragraph style*.

style sheet   A technology that enables a Web author to more precisely control the appearance of a Web page and to easily apply and modify that design in multiple pages.

subtree   A collection of pages in a *FrontPage Web site* that branches off another level of pages at least one level below the top page.

symbol   A character that's not on the keyboard, such as a copyright symbol. In *FrontPage 2003*, you add symbols to your pages from a special *dialog box*.

T

table   A box or grid used to arrange text or pictures in neat rows and columns; often used in *FrontPage 2003* to organize the entire layout of the page.

tag   A code in the *HTML* language.

target   See *bookmark*.

task   In *FrontPage 2003*, an activity assigned to an individual as part of coordinating a multi-author Web authoring project, usually over a *network* on which *FrontPage 2003* is installed.

task pane   In *FrontPage 2003* and all *Office 2003* programs, a panel along the right side of the screen that opens to help you perform certain tasks, such as opening a Web site to edit or applying a *theme*.

template   A preformatted Web page (containing sample text and pictures) that a Web author uses to model a new page on.

theme   In *FrontPage 2003*, a set of formatting instructions governing the *background*, *fonts*, colors, and button styles in a page. Themes provide a fast way to design a page or change a design and to apply a matching design to multiple pages in a *FrontPage Web site*.

thumbnail   In a Web page, a small, low-resolution picture that, when clicked, opens a full-size image of the same picture. Thumbnails are used in *photo galleries*.

title   The name that identifies a particular Web page. A Web page's title appears in the title bar at the top of the *browser* window.

toolbar   In a program, a row of icons or buttons, usually near the top of the program's window, that you can click to perform common tasks.

U-V

Undo   A feature of *FrontPage 2003* and some other programs that enables you to reverse an action you performed if you change your mind.

upload   The act of copying information to a server computer from your computer. See also *download*.

URL   Short for *uniform* (or *universal*) *resource locator*. A method of standardizing the addresses of different types of Internet resources so that they can all be accessed easily from within a Web browser; for example, the address http://quepublishing.com is a URL.

view   A particular set of information displayed in a certain way by *FrontPage 2003* that varies based on what you are doing. In Design view, you edit your page; in Preview view, you test it.

visitor   A casual way a Web author may refer to the people who will access his or her creations through the *Internet* or an *intranet*.

Visual Basic   A multipurpose programming language from Microsoft, often used for Web page *scripts* and for automating tasks in *Office 2003* programs.

W-X

web   See *FrontPage Web site* or *World Wide Web*.

Web site   A group of individual Web pages linked together into a single, multipage document. The term *Web site* also is sometimes used to describe a whole Web *server* or all pages on a particular *domain*.

Webmaster   The person responsible for the management and maintenance of a particular Web page or Web site. Sometimes (but not always) also the Web page's author.

wizard   Automated routines, used throughout Windows, for conveniently performing a step-by-step procedure, such as installing *FrontPage 2003*.

World Wide Web (WWW or Web)
A set of Internet computers and services that provide an easy-to-use system for finding information and moving among resources. Do not confuse with *FrontPage Web site*.

WYSIWYG   Short for "What You See Is What You Get," a way of describing Web-authoring programs such as *FrontPage 2003*, which show you the page as it will appear online while you work on it.

Y-Z

Yahoo!   A popular search engine.

Index

Symbols